"AND SO—THEY INDICTED ME!"

"AND SO—THEY INDICTED ME!"

A Story of New Deal Persecution

by J. EDWARD JONES

1 9 3 8

J. EDWARD JONES PUBLISHING CORPORATION

New York

PRINTED IN THE UNITED STATES OF AMERICA

"Arbitrary power and the rule of
the Constitution cannot both exist."
The Supreme Court of the United States

"AND SO—THEY INDICTED ME!"

PREFACE

Nowhere in the world today is the purpose of government so dedicated to principles for the protection of individual freedom and liberty against the tyrannical oppressions of political usurpation, as in America. The great institutions of government created by the Constitution of the United States stand as mighty bulwarks, not only for individual freedom in this country, but also as outstanding examples of justice to all other peoples.

For in the ultimate, the American Individual, not the American State, is supreme. There is only one thing more powerful in the American Democracy than the American Government itself, and that is American Public Opinion—that composite majority of individual ideas held by the society which supports the State. As against the American Government itself, American Public Opinion will prevail—for such opinion, under our form of government, can change the policies and

7

purposes of the government and direct them at will.

Before the establishment of the American Democracy, the history of world affairs was a sorry record of constant impositions and restrictions upon human liberties and freedom by officialdoms which then held the ordinary individual to be a mere pawn, his personal rights and liberties subjected always to the supreme rule and arbitrary power of the State. With profound wisdom and remarkable foresight, our founding fathers provided us with a governmental system which not only proclaimed our nation a haven for individual liberty, but, indeed, created a three-fold system of checks and balances within our own governmental structure to defend against attempted encroachments upon the rights and liberties of our own citizens even by officials and agencies of our own government.

This book is a record of factual events which, thanks to the Supreme Court of the United States, prove that individual freedom still lives in this country and that government of the people under the American system really functions for their protection. It reveals the government itself, through its admirable system of checks and balances, acting judicially to expel from the executive branch of its own structure influences that would submerge human liberties. In face of a tyrannical abuse of

power arbitrarily exercised through a usurpation
of unwarranted and illegally assumed authority on
the part of officials of the executive department,
the record shows the American judiciary supreme
in its lofty purpose and firmly set against new and
alien conceptions of governmental principles. It
reveals the fact, also, that political graft and extortion cannot control the American people by putting a price tag on all of their public officials—
even if petty vindictiveness may absorb the mentalities of some of them.

In order to make clear the significance of the
events herein treated, I should like the reader of
these pages to remove, in his appraisal, my own personality from the J. Edward Jones about whom the
facts are recorded. It is wise, I think, for one to
consider that the things which happened to me
well might happen to anybody else. But so long
as citizens of our country courageously strike back
at evils encountered in the maladministration of our
government, justice will prevail. A citizenry apa-
thetic to conditions dangerously threatening its
own liberty is not deserving of the honor of such
sacred possession. It is un-American for a citizen
to fear personal consequences when he faces an attack upon his basic beliefs regarding his rights as a
citizen.

Many of my friends and well-wishers have advised me against publishing this book. Frankly, they fear that the publication of the events herein recorded might provoke anew a series of vicious, vindictive attacks against me by certain persons in government who might venture any lengths to accomplish my destruction. In acknowledging, with appreciation and sympathetic understanding, such splendid consideration for my welfare, I must state that I sincerely feel it to be my duty, as a citizen, to reveal for public digestion, information concerning a status of affairs I consider to be subversive of good government in this country. I believe, also, that one possessed of information of the character of that with which I am possessed, is duty bound to expose it to the end that knowledge of the conditions thus brought to light may aid to remedy such conditions. How can the art of government progress if evils in government be blanketed by a cloak of secrecy and shrouded with fear and trembling?

I assume full personal responsibility for everything stated in this book. I, myself, have written the whole of it; and I know it to be all true and capable of being proved, if any need to prove it, perchance, should arise. If the truthfulness of the story told in this book be seriously questioned, I shall adduce proper evidence to support it. I have at hand excellent material of even more sensational character than that so far used—material which well could fill many other chapters; but I believe the book, as written, will suffice to serve, what I shall ask my readers to believe to be, a sincere effort toward something constructive—not destructive.

J. EDWARD JONES

New York, N. Y.
March, 1938

CONTENTS

Chapter		Page
	Preface	7
I	"I'm for Roosevelt"	15
II	The New Deal Looks to Oil	19
III	Introduction to the Governors' Oil Conference	26
IV	First Gun	34
V	Meet Mr. Ickes	43
VI	Meet Mr. Roosevelt	55
VII	The Genesis of NRA—Its Character	63
VIII	New Deal Policeman	94
IX	Let the Seller Beware!	104
X	Mr. Flynn Goes to Town	125
XI	New Deal's "Most Effective Weapon"	131
XII	"Arbitrary Power" vs. "Rule of the Constitution"	148
XIII	"Truth in Securities"	165
XIV	More "Truth in Securities"	176
XV	The Supreme Court Speaks!	193
XVI	New Deal at Work	201
XVII	New Dealirium	207
XVIII	Books for Sale!	222
XIX	*Pax Vobiscum*	243

"I'm for Roosevelt"

I was one of those Americans who voted for Franklin D. Roosevelt in the Presidential Election of 1932. I was more than that—I was one of those enrolled Republican voters who helped him to win. I believed implicitly in his pre-election promises. Mr. Roosevelt, to me, gave every indication of being a leader possessed of political and social philosophies which I thought, could they be put into effect, would be representative of the beginning of a new and better era in the lives of men.

As the Governor swung into his first presidential campaign—attacking, as he did, the old regime for its alleged favors to the entrenched monopolies, and posing as the fearless champion of his "forgotten man," my enthusiasm for his seeming courage in a battle to set aright economic evils was as boundless as was my unlimited admiration for the man— a man whom I deemed a real Crusader, soundly supported by great ideals for that much desired

"new and better social order." The genuine hope
which Mr. Roosevelt's promises and his stated position as a candidate instilled in me became, as the
campaign progressed, a firm belief, before he was
elected, that, given a chance, he certainly would
prove to be one man upon whom the people
could depend to restore opportunity in life to the
individual and to restrict the practices of the powerful in unfair exploitation of the common man. I
believe my thought of Mr. Roosevelt in that connection was the thought of millions of other Americans who had been attracted by the promises of
as charming and gracious a personality as ever hyp-
notized an audience—be it street corner or convention hall calibre.

The ideals pictured by Mr. Roosevelt in his campaign appealed to all classes of the people. Both to
the intelligent voter and the unthinking masses,
new visions appeared. Out of what seemed to be
sincere and courageous campaign battle, beautiful
abstractions readily became promises of practical
realities and—behold!—now the ravages of the de-
pression were revealed clearly as the fruits of Republican wickedness linked, of course, to that class
of society hitherto regarded as successful people
but now frowned upon, later, indeed, to be counted
as the hated "economic royalists!"

On March 4th, 1933, I thrilled greatly in listening to the new President's Inaugural Address as it came over the radio. The triumphal tone and seemingly sympathetic understanding which characterized that address, clearly signified to me that the people of America had rightly chosen a man who had correctly analyzed their problems, who had his finger on their real cause and who was possessed of the courage, determination and ability necessary to solve those problems in quick fashion. True— the public did not know the nature of the prescription which was to be administered to cure its ills, but tremendous confidence born by the mere existence of the new administration produced a hypnosis which made for progress even prior to New Deal performance.

Psychologists of the future will find rare and fertile source of interesting material in studying the period 1932-1933 to determine the causes which contributed to shape public opinion of the time. Well may they speculate upon the reasons why a great people blindly followed an undefined abstraction dangled with soul-inspiring effect before their imaginative eyes as a promised cure for the most practical of problems! Strange fiction may they write of the readiness with which the great American Democracy gave up—and gladly—

sweeping authority over its people, to make of its president the strongest, most powerful autocrat the world has ever seen in government!

But just as the public mind was surcharged with hope and confidence—with no idea of a *modus operandi* for the accomplishment of anything—so was the New Deal administration equally charged and champing at the bit for action in some direction. However, there was no signpost pointing the way over any roads America previously had traveled.

In such state of affairs, I felt certain, now the inauguration was over, that steps quickly would be taken by Washington to solve the highly controversial problems of the petroleum industry, with which I always had been identified.

CHAPTER II

The New Deal Looks to Oil

In a letter written to me during his first presidential campaign, Mr. Roosevelt had promised that while addressing the nation, he would outline his policies with respect to the American oil problem. I thought nothing of his failure to do so, however, since the progress of the campaign revealed his seeming determination to restrict the unfair privileges of big business in all lines of industry. I knew from my own exhaustive research, over a period of years, in the field of petroleum economics —having been commissioned to represent my home State of Kansas in preparing analyses of petroleum problems and having appeared before various committees of both houses of Congress as a representative of the so-called "independents" of the industry —that the evils in the American Economy which Mr. Roosevelt had attacked were glaringly present in oil and representing problems demanding of solution. In no industry did the individual, independent

operator need more protection against monopoly
than did the small American oil operator. As a matter of fact, in 1932, the "forgotten man" in the
petroleum industry was just about ready to be bur-
ied as the unknown soldier in that great American war between the individual and the predatory
interests in business.

And so, the New Deal Administration, taking
office on March 4th, 1933, in one of its very first
acts, plunged headlong into the pool of oil troubles. Within a few days after the inauguration,
the President's new Secretary of the Interior, one
Harold Loy Ickes, issued a call for a "Governors'
Oil Conference" to be held in Washington on the
27th day of March for the announced purpose of
"solving the problems" of the petroleum industry.
The principal problem to be "grappled with," said
the Secretary in his "Call," was one of "overproduction" of crude oil in this country.

To any student of economics, the "solving the
problems" of any industry is a major undertaking
that should be attempted only by experts soundly
grounded not only in comprehensive knowledge
of the basic facts of the industry under study, but
also in a thorough understanding of all the elements
at play to influence the fundamental economic factors of supply, demand and price. Without such

equipment, attempt to function wisely toward the alleviation of industrial evils is pure folly. But excessive vanity of man always inclines dangerously toward folly!

By way of giving an authoritative tone to the statement made in the Call to the Conference, that "overproduction" of crude oil was the problem to be "grappled with," Mr. Ickes boldly stated that the production of crude oil in this country approximated 2,500,000 barrels daily whereas, he said, the nation's consumption requirements were but 2,000,-000 barrels daily. The "Call" therefore implied a bad supply and demand balance for crude oil and immediately created an issue of first magnitude, indicating strong need for corrective and controlling measures. And the New Deal Administration stood ready—determined to correct and to control!

Of the forty-eight American states, twenty-one of them produce crude oil in varying quantities. All of these twenty-one states, if not, indeed, the entire forty-eight, are vitally interested in the welfare of the petroleum industry and the policies which determine its conduct. However, in attempting to solve the problems of the nation's third largest industry, Mr. Ickes first invited the Governors of only four states to his "Governors' Oil Conference." Yet my disappointment at the undue

restriction of the proposed conference did not equal
my great dismay at what I knew to be a misstate-
ment in the "Call" regarding the relationship of
supply and demand of crude oil.

For years, in spite of great propaganda to the
contrary, production of crude oil in America had
been so restricted artificially under the imposition
of control by the governments of the oil states, that
we actually had an *underproduction,* not an overproduction, of crude oil in this country. *The deficiency, amounting to many hundred millions of
barrels, had been supplied steadily by three or four
major oil concerns through the importation of
cheap foreign oils from properties owned by those
organizations in foreign countries, principally
Venezuela.* These importations were being forced
upon the American oil industry against the strong
protests of the independent producers whose American oil wells were forced to shut down. Of necessity, the supplying of the market then was handed
over, gratis, to those few oil organizations in position to obtain oil from their foreign fields.

The controversy over this situation had become
sharp to a point of viciousness between the independents and the major oil concerns who both
monopolized the markets and propagandized the
public into the firm belief that the one big problem

of the industry was *too much oil*. This was verily believed by the average man although, as I have stated, the fact was that we had in our country a condition of restricted production—an *under*production which contributed to a deficiency in our domestic supply so as to create a tremendous volume of good business denied the independent producer but reserved exclusively for those few companies who could monopolize the importations from their foreign holdings. Good results from an effective propaganda!

The old Hoover-Wilbur administration had favored the major oil company side of the controversy. Mr. Wilbur probably best summarized his policy by stating that if he "were the landlord of this country," he would shut-in all American oil wells and force our consumption requirements to be filled from wells in foreign countries. The policy enraged the independents of the industry and caused them, throughout the country, to support Mr. Roosevelt.

On the day following press announcements of the Conference invitation by Mr. Ickes, who, by such invitation, gave evidence that he intended to follow what we independents had fought for years as misguided public policy toward oil, I received telegrams from all sections of the oil territory—as far west as California—urging me to do something toward extending the scope of the Conference. I was urged to set Mr. Ickes aright on the real facts concerning the supply and demand of petroleum, and to point out to him the disastrous influence of monopoly in creating a false issue and in spreading false propaganda to mask its real purpose. Therefore, on March 16, 1933, I dispatched identical telegrams to all the governors of oil producing states, who had not been invited to the Conference. The telegrams read as follows:

NEW SECRETARY INTERIOR ICKES HAS CALLED
CONFERENCE GOVERNORS TEXAS OKLAHOMA
KANSAS CALIFORNIA FOR MARCH TWENTY
SEVENTH TO DISCUSS PROBLEMS PETROLEUM
STOP YOUR STATE IS PROSPECTIVE PRODUCER
OF PETROLEUM AND IS VITALLY AFFECTED BY
PROBLEMS PETROLEUM INDUSTRY STOP SUCH
ISSUES AS REVOLVE AROUND MONOPOLISTIC
PRACTICES THROUGH UNFAIR COMPETITIVE
METHODS REGULATION OF PRODUCTION PRICE
FIXING GOVERNMENTAL ACTIVITY RESPECT-
ING INDUSTRIAL CONDUCT ETCETERA WILL
BE TREATED AT CONFERENCE STOP THESE MAT-
TERS SHOULD NOT BE DISCUSSED FOR SOLU-
TION WITHOUT YOUR STATE BEING REPRE-
SENTED THEREFORE URGE YOU APPEAL SECRE-
TARY INTERIOR IMMEDIATELY FOR REPRESEN-
TATION AT THAT CONFERENCE STOP RESPECT-
FULLY

J. EDWARD JONES
342 Madison Avenue
New York City

Thereupon, something must have happened, for about two days later the press carried announcements that several additional governors had been invited by Mr. Ickes to attend his Conference. The Honorable Ruby Laffoon, Governor of Kentucky, appointed me to represent the State of Kentucky. Other individuals representing both independents and majors were invited to attend as was also the powerful American Petroleum Institute—sometimes called "the mouthpiece of monopoly."

As news of the new complexion of the coming Conference permeated the industry, a general recognition matured that this first New Deal step in the direction of oil was going to be an important step. Data were hurriedly collected, charts and graphs were prepared, meetings were scheduled, and Washington became the Mecca for hundreds of oil men from all sections of the United States. We all had confidence and hope in the New Deal Administration, and were determined to lay all the facts of the case before the Conference.

CHAPTER III

Introduction to the Governors'
Oil Conference

The crowd of oil men arrived in Washington a few days prior to Monday, March 27th. They held their customary conferences and inevitably formed their two opposing camps. The field became one of battle—not of peace—as the forces of the independent individual marshalled against the powerful phalanxes of organized big business. The Governors' Oil Conference of the New Deal Administration quickly crystallized into a picture that represented in the concrete all the elements of industrial strife that Mr. Roosevelt had so vividly portrayed during his campaign. The eye of the American public, through the lens of Mr. Roosevelt's political camera, had been focused upon the outlines of evil influence in our economic life; here was the actual grouping of all the characters of a major industry in a panoramic war film that covered everything!

And there was plot in the play; for two great

opposing forces contended with each other in almost desperate effort, each to jockey itself into the position most likely to impress a new and inexperienced political machine. One side, supported by corporations owning and controlling billions of wealth but fearful of the destructive competition of myriads of "little men" businesses, desired Federal control of the productive processes of the industry. They desired this because the lesson had been learned that unwise and unknowing officialdom, somehow or other, could be depended upon to control always in the interest of the powerful in business. And the powerful in the oil business wanted to choke off the production of its independent competitors. Otherwise, that deficiency in domestic production, which necessitated huge foreign oil importations, could not be created.

The other side represented what America knows as rugged individualism in business. And "rugged" is a good word to describe the qualities an individual oil operator must possess if he is to exist at all. Courage, strength of character, the pioneer spirit, enthusiasm, cheerfulness in face of dire trouble, hope, determination—all these one finds in the individualism that has pushed the oil frontiers to such extents that in a few years the petroleum industry has become the country's third largest. Competition? They meet it; they create it; they live on it as the life of their trade. Control? What is meant by the word "control"? Rugged individualism in oil despised monopolistic control of business, was distrustful of any plan that vested control of the affairs of industry in the hands of a powerful Federal bureaucracy. The individual oil operator owed his very existence to the competition he always had been free to create in doing battle against "control" in business. He disliked the word and all it implied. He was a natural and genuine champion of the *laissez-faire* principle of trade. For years he had fought monopolistic influence and power, and Mr. Roosevelt's entire campaign had implied that he intended, if elected, to take up the cudgels and put the force of government behind the effort to destroy "control" of the affairs of industry and to permit free, competitive, individual enterprise.

At the Governors' Oil Conference the rugged individualist desired that the new government be apprised of the facts of the oil controversy. Moreover, he wanted that protection and freedom from the powerful monopolistic control of his affairs which he expected the New Deal would give him— once it had learned the truth of the situation. President Roosevelt's campaign speeches still were ringing in his ears. The new President, he felt sure, was his champion. Mr. Roosevelt must not be allowed to get off on the wrong track at the very outset of his new administration! That was the cry throughout the ranks!

On Sunday morning, immediately preceding the day set for the opening of the Conference, Mr. Wirt Franklin, President of the Independent Petroleum Association of America, called to order in the Chinese Room of the Mayflower Hotel, a meeting which had been heralded as one to be attended by the independents of the industry. It was understood that at the meeting the position of the independents would be formulated so that, on the morrow, the Conference could be notified of their generally accepted views. If the position of the independents could be made known and recorded in some sort of an "official" manner at the very outset of the Conference, it was felt that argument and debate as to what that position was, would not mar the hoped-for success of the great meeting of the governors and their representatives.

Such reasoning seemed logical enough. Many of the independents, however, looked upon the meeting with considerable skepticism and no little misgivings since a rumor persisted to the effect that this Independent Petroleum Association of America, of which Mr. Wirt Franklin was president, and

which presumed to speak the independent side of
the oil controversy was, in fact, a "decoy of monopoly." Nevertheless, in a genuine spirit of co-
operation we independents made it our business to
go to Mr. Franklin's meeting of independent American oil men in the Chinese Room of the Mayflower
Hotel on that Sunday morning preceding the opening of Mr. Ickes' Governors' Oil Conference—a
Conference called to "grapple with" a problem
which did not, in fact, exist, and to "solve the
problems" of a major industry (presumably at one
sitting, immediately following the opening speech
of the new Secretary of the Interior).

My Director of Research, Mr. William J. Kemnitzer, a group of representatives from California,
Texas and Louisiana, and I, upon entering the room,
were somewhat surprised to note that nearly all the
seating space of one half of the room was occupied
by representatives of major oil concerns and the
American Petroleum Institute, whose membership
and financial support depended upon the oil combine which the independents opposed as a matter
of policy. Independents filled the remaining seats.
It appeared to be the old story—a meeting of independents packed by representatives of the majors!

Mr. Wirt Franklin, as was his wont, made a long
and emotional speech. He stated that we were

present to formulate a policy that could be announced to the Governors' Oil Conference as the determined position of the independents of the industry. He wanted no discord in his meeting but insisted upon results! And, shaking with emotion, he demanded that any person opposing the contemplated action leave the room!

The head of Mr. Franklin's affiliated Texas concern which, by the way, Texas State officials later exposed, made a speech in which he decried what he insisted was a condition of "overproduction" in the industry and called for more control of the productive processes. Several other well-known henchmen of the "monopoly in oil" then took the floor and reiterated this demand for more "control" of the affairs of the industry. Representatives of independents from California, Texas and Louisiana began, now and then, to shout questions at the speakers as, one after the other, they were recognized by the chair and proceeded always to claim "overproduction" and to demand "control."

Within a short time, we were dumbfounded upon seeing the genial Mr. Bill Boyd, Executive Vice President of the American Petroleum Institute, arise in this "independent" meeting! And, as he stood surrounded by numerous officers and employees of the largest of the nation's oil concerns, he began to read a prepared resolution which he moved as one to be adopted as the policy of the meeting! The resolution embodied the old thesis of the oil combine, deplored the alleged "overproduction" situation, called for control of the production of crude oil insofar as American oil wells were concerned but, significantly, made no mention of any control of foreign operations or any cessation of continued importations of foreign oils.

Although at times I had been quietly urged to do so, I had taken no part in the proceedings that had preceded the offering of the resolution. At the conclusion of Mr. Boyd's remarks, however, my friends literally pushed me from my seat and toward the front of the room. Naturally, I then became involved in the debate.

I discussed the relationship of supply and demand of crude oil, pointed out with the aid of elaborate charts and statistics of the United States Bureau of Mines that the "overproduction" bugaboo was a myth, revealed that attempts toward artificial restriction of production had previously had an adverse effect upon price, argued against the creation of a false issue of "overproduction" when no such condition existed, urged the meeting not to be a party to the misleading of the New Administration in that respect, challenged the oil monopoly to meet the real issue of the industry, chided their representatives for packing an independent meeting and for taking part in a "steam-roller" proceeding to control the functioning of that meeting, pointed out the adverse effect on public opinion if the Boyd resolution were to be adopted, and finally notified those present that if the resolution passed, I proposed to take the floor at the Governors' Oil Conference the next day and, as the representative of the Governor of the State of Kentucky, notify the Conference of the "packing" of the Franklin meeting—who was present at it, and who had proposed and forced through the objectionable resolution.

Over the angry protests of the enraged Mr. Franklin, debate degenerated into argument between the two forces. Through the aid of the Chair, however, the question finally was put to the "packed" house, whereupon the California delegation, which occupied front rows of seats, headed by Mr. John B. Elliott, their able leader, arose and started to file from the room. Men from Texas and Louisiana fell in with the procession as it moved up the center aisle, and other friends, along with me, joined them. We all left the meeting in disappointment and in disgust.

We learned, of course, that those who remained passed the resolution.

CHAPTER IV

First Gun

The following morning we found that the Washington Press, and many other important papers throughout the country, featured the break in the ranks of oil men as represented by the "bolt" of the independents. Hotel corridors buzzed with speculation as to what might happen at two o'clock that afternoon when the Conference proper convened. Before noon, report had it that the big companies would seize upon the situation as an opportunity to throw another big oil scare about "overproduction" and waste of one of the nation's important and irreplaceable natural resources. The fact that huge importations of cheap foreign oil were being poured by the large companies upon an alleged "overproduced" country was to be kept as quiet as possible; the New Deal Administration was to be given an excellent opportunity to "control" the productive processes of a great industry and—with an eye to the times and to the ambitious march toward power of some of those newcomers, girded for their first time with the authority of government—a plan of control was to be suggested that envisaged the appointment of a dictator for the petroleum industry!

A few of us who understood the strategy of the oil monopoly in its efforts toward moulding public opinion and influencing the acts of public officials, realized the power of such a program. A sensational speech at the Conference by some vice-president or chairman of any big oil company, could easily create the news to cause public concern, and the appeal to the ego of ambitious officialdom certainly was present in the scheme; for what a field in which a new official might ride—saddled on the horse of his imagination, charging through a nightmare of fear, and saving, through the route of governmental control of production, the drowning public from a deluge of oil!

The independents of the industry had the biggest job of their careers. It was up to them to expose this "overproduction" myth, to reveal the truth of the situation, to unmask the false hypothesis of their powerful and influential adversaries, and to lay before the sympathetic New Deal Government the real facts of the oil problem. And some of us had those facts—irrefutable and unquestionably authentic!

We had not considered, however, the possibility of losing our battle through the enthronement of vanity and foolish ambition upon a foundation of admitted ignorance. Neither were we suspicious of trickery, nor did we dream of underhanded attack.

The hour for the meeting of the governors and their representatives approached, and a half-dozen taxicabs took a number of my close friends and me to the Department of the Interior Building, where a great auditorium was to house several hundred men of the oil industry.

As we walked down the corridor toward the entrance of the auditorium which already had begun to fill with the representatives, we noticed, gathered in a large crowd and in front of the door, many of those familiar faces who had been present on the day before as our adversaries in the Franklin meeting. A very noticeable bustling in this crowd was evidenced as we pushed our way forward to the door. I carried in my hand a letter which read as follows:

> Commonwealth of Kentucky
> United We Stand
> Divided We Fall

Commonwealth of Kentucky
EXECUTIVE CHAMBER

RUBY LAFFOON
Governor

Frankfort

March 20, 1933

To the Honorable
The Secretary of the Interior
Washington, D. C.

Sir:

Mr. J. Edward Jones, the bearer hereof, is the representative of the Governor of Kentucky, duly appointed by him to represent the State of Kentucky at the Governors' Oil Conference to be held in Washington, D. C., on March 27, 1933, which has been called by the Secretary of the Interior for that date.

Mr. Jones will be admitted to said Conference as the duly authorized representative of Kentucky.

Very truly yours,

RUBY LAFFOON
Governor of Kentucky

ATTEST:

Sara W. Mahan
Secretary of State

SEAL:

> Commonwealth
> of
> Kentucky
> United We Stand
> Divided—We Fall

As I started to put my foot across the very threshold of the door, a young man whom I never before had seen stepped quickly to the front of me, stopped me, and asked if I were J. Edward Jones. On receiving his answer he handed me a telegram and remained standing before me in my path. I fell back, as did my friends who were with me, opened the telegram and received the surprise of my life! Governor Laffoon of Kentucky had cancelled my credentials!

The crowd of hangers-on tittered as they watched me read and re-read, without, at first, comprehending the telegram, which was as follows:

WESTERN UNION

Received at Interior Department Bldg. Washington, D. C.
1933 MAR 27 PM 1 01

WN54 40—FRANKFORT KY 27 1141A

J EDWARD JONES CARE CONFERENCE OF OIL
    MEN CARE SECY OF INTERIOR

I HAVE BEEN IMPORTUNED BY KENTUCKY OIL
MEN TO APPOINT A RESIDENT OF KENTUCKY
TO REPRESENT KENTUCKY AT THE OIL CON-
FERENCE AND HAVE ACCORDINGLY APPOINT-
ED MR M W SHIARELLA OF OWENSBORO KY
YOUR AUTHORITY TO REPRESENT KENTUCKY
THEREFORE IS REVOKED

RUBY LAFFOON GOV OF KENTUCKY

Delegations from several states headed by my

friends, Jack Blalock and Joe Danciger of Texas, Major Parten from Louisiana and John Elliott of California, walked with me down the corridor in hurried and excited comment as to what had contributed to cause this humiliating slight to me. All urged me to telephone Governor Laffoon, in Frankfort, to obtain an immediate explanation.

I reached the Governor, told him I had just received his telegram and asked him to give me the reasons which had prompted him to dismiss me. The Governor informed me that he was not familiar with the oil controversy; that he had not realized that there was going to be any division of opinion at the Conference; that he did not want to be put in the position of fighting the new administration; and, finally, that since ten o'clock of the night before he literally had been besieged with a deluge of telegrams and telephone calls from at least seven towns and cities of Kentucky imploring him to appoint as Kentucky's representative at the Conference, a resident of the state!

I thanked the Governor for his explanation and for the courtesy he had shown me in our conversation and respectfully accepted, of course, his wishes. I advised him, however, that opposing the new administration was the farthest thing from my mind; that I saw no reason for such an attitude on my part as I was, so he knew, a supporter of the independent side of the oil controversy; and that we independents were in Washington to help the administration in a proper understanding of the real oil issue, not to fight it. Governor Laffoon then hospitably invited me to visit him the next time I found myself in the State of Kentucky.

My independent friends and associates thereupon refused to take any part in the Conference and we all repaired to another auditorium of the building where resolutions were passed expressing indignation for the treatment to which I had been subjected, condemning the non-representative character of the Conference, and appointing a committee which was instructed to wait upon the Secretary of the Interior for the purpose of requesting permission to lay before him the independents' view of petroleum troubles.

Meanwhile the conference proper had heard Secretary Ickes' address, copies of which were obtained and distributed among those present at our own meeting which continued in session until our committee had communicated with the Secretary immediately after he had left the main conference. Mr. Ickes very kindly consented to meet with us at ten o'clock the following morning, Tuesday the 28th, and a Committee of five was appointed to

confer with him, I being included on the membership of that Committee. A resolution was passed
authorizing the forwarding of the following telegram to the Governor of Kentucky:

WESTERN UNION

WASHINGTON DC MARCH 27 1933
HONORABLE RUBY LAFFOON
GOVERNOR OF KENTUCKY   FRANKFORT KENTUCKY
YOUR APPARENTLY INNOCENT ACTION IN RE-
VOKING THE AUTHORITY OF MR J EDWARD
JONES TO REPRESENT YOU AT THE GOVERN-
ORS OIL CONFERENCE BEFORE THE SECRETARY
OF INTERIOR CAME AS A GREAT SHOCK TO
MR JONES PERSONALLY AND TO ALL TRUE
AND UNCONTROLLED OIL OPERATORS FROM
EVERY SECTION OF THE UNITED STATES HIS
MASTERY OF OIL ECONOMICS TRUE BASIS
FACTS AND FIGURES AND FUNDAMENTAL
PRINCIPLES AND HIS CAPABLE AND FORCEFUL
PRESENTATION OF THEM BEFORE A LARGE
GATHERING OF REPRESENTATIVES OF THE OIL
INDUSTRY GAINED THE RESPECT AND ADMIRA-
TION OF HIS AUDIENCE THE TELEGRAMS AND
LETTERS SENT YOU TO THE EFFECT THAT HE
WAS NOT THOROUGHLY FULFILLING HIS MIS-
SION FROM ANY POINT OF VIEW INDICATES
THE VICIOUS METHODS TO WHICH THE MONOP-
OLISTIC ELEMENT IN THE OIL INDUSTRY WILL
STOOP TO DISCREDIT AND DESTROY AN HON-
EST AND FEARLESS REPRESENTATIVE OF THE
PEOPLE WE FEEL IT A MATTER OF SIMPLE JUS-
TICE AND OUR PLAIN DUTY TO INFORM YOU
OF THE SOURCE OF HIS OPPOSITION AND CON-
SIDER SUCH UNDERHANDED ACTIVITY ON THE

PART OF PREDATORY INTERESTS THE HIGHEST
FLATTERY THAT COULD BE PAID THE ABILITY
OF MR JONES AS AN ILLUSTRATION OF THE EF-
FICIENT MANNER IN WHICH HE WAS REPRE-
SENTING THE GREAT STATE OF KENTUCKY WE
ARE SENDING YOU A COPY OF HIS ADDRESS
WHICH MONOPOLY SUCCEEDED TEMPORARILY
IN SUPPRESSING AS A RESULT OF THEIR MIS-
REPRESENTATIONS TO YOU RESPECTFULLY RES-
OLUTION ADOPTED BY COMMITTEE REPRESENT-
ING INDEPENDENT OIL PRODUCESRS OF UNITED
STATES ASSEMBLED IN WASHINGTON

JOHN B ELLIOTT LOS ANGELES CALIF CHAIRMAN
JACK BLALOCK MARSHALL TEXAS SECRETARY

CHAPTER V

Meet Mr. Ickes

Mr. Ickes received us on Tuesday morning in a small room of the Interior Building. He sat behind a huge desk and to his left sat Mr. E. S. Rochester, Secretary of the Federal Oil Conservation Board.

Our spokesman, Mr. John B. Elliott, California's leader, began, in most polite and respectful manner, to explain to Mr. Ickes our reasons for having made the request for a special meeting with him. As Mr. Elliott warmed to his subject, referring to the sharpness of the oil controversy, he made reference to the packing by the majors of the Franklin meeting which, he stated, had been called as one for independents only. He advised the Secretary of the fact that the resolutions passed by that meeting had been proposed and supported, in fact, by the major concerns and their henchmen. He also declared that the Governors' Oil Conference itself was not at all representative of the rank and file of the petroleum industry, but was, on the contrary, principally composed of the dominating monopolistic organizations of the Industry.

As Mr. Ickes listened to Mr. Elliott, he very definitely began to exhibit a demeanor of anger and belligerency. His face became drawn and almost white. Finally he cut short Mr. Elliott by bursting out, as he turned directly toward me, that "if it hadn't been for Mr. Jones," the Conference would not have been so big anyway. "Mr. Jones," he stated, "went over my head by sending a telegram which implied I had slighted the governors by not inviting them all." He said that he had thereupon invited more governors, as well as several associations of oil men, including the Executive Committee of the American Petroleum Institute. He then complained that "you independents" had "come down here" and caused trouble by bolting a meeting of oil men on Sunday so that "all the papers" on Monday morning carried news of a breakup of the Conference even before it had been officially called to order by him. Mr. Ickes was obviously a very wrought-up and angry man as he snapped his words in a severe, almost lecturing style.

The very much surprised Mr. Elliott, ignorant of the point of Mr. Ickes' adverse criticism of me, mumbled that he knew nothing of the matter, that he could not "speak for Mr. Jones," but that since I was present he would yield the floor to me.

As I arose, I faced a man whom I fully desired to aid in what I knew to be a complex and difficult undertaking insofar as his job toward the petroleum industry was concerned. Although I never before had heard of his connection with any great accomplishments, I instinctively was most friendly and sympathetically inclined toward him because he had been selected as a Cabinet officer of that New Deal Administration in which I had so much genuine hope and confidence. I was certain that, once in Washington and at the seat of our government— now newly dedicated to principles affording protection and aid to the individual "forgotten man" in his long struggle toward real freedom of competitive enterprise—I would find all the prominent New Deal representatives, at least, of a democratic attitude, representative of the appeal which had won the tremendous support of the public in the recent election.

I began, in very calm and reserved manner, to utter an expression to the effect that I did not then recall the exact wording of my telegram to the governors but that I knew I had not intended to convey any slight to the esteemed Secretary. Mr. Ickes, with whitened face and his finger shaking at

me, exploded that he knew well what was in the
telegram and that he then had a copy of one on
his desk before him! He thereupon appeared to
slump into a sulk of seeming juvenility and sat star-
ing at papers on his desk, but not making any attempt at all to enlighten the audience as to the
nature of the telegram which seemed so to have
upset his mental poise and equilibrium.

As far as dignity permitted, I gave expression to
my regrets at the circumstances. I told Mr. Ickes,
however, that I felt I had been within my proper
province in my communication to the governors,
particularly since he had made misstatements concerning facts relating to a very important matter
and that by virtue of his misstatements, a false issue
had been created in the industry. I then told the
Secretary that I desired to ask him two questions.
He angrily nodded a sullen assent.

"First," I said, "I should like respectfully to ask
whether you are an oil man and whether you are
familiar with the statistical position of the petroleum industry." He banged his fist as he roused
from his slump, almost bellowing, "I am not an
oil man and I don't know a damn thing about the
oil business!"

I don't know the influence which prompted it,
but my mind, in a split fraction of a second, quickly

glimpsed, in panorama, several of our noted representatives of greatness who had sat in Washington during our history—themselves famed for a wisdom which always was tempered with, if not, indeed, actuated by calmness of mind, tolerance of spirit, mentalities open not only to helpful suggestions but also, indeed, to argument. The profundity of Lincolnesque thinking, for instance, did not go along with explosive and vindictive thrusts shot out in defense of any silly vanity. What a chapter on character this demonstration before me was writing!

I decided to appeal—and to manhood!

"My second question, Mr. Secretary, is this: If I can show you, as a man to man proposition, that you made a mistake in the statistics you quoted in your Call to the Conference and that the figures as you used them the better could have been reversed to come nearer facts, and if I could convince you that you had by your mistake created a false issue as the very basis for your own Conference"— I continued—"I had intended to ask a question—but I will not do so: I will state to you that I believe that if I could, as man to man, so convince you, you would retract your statement which I happen to know was given widespread publicity by all three wire services throughout the entire country."

Mr. Ickes' demeanor suddenly changed. His angry and bellicose attitude at once gave way to an almost inquiring curiosity. "What is wrong with my figures?" he asked. I replied that he had stated to the governors and, through his publicity release to the American public, that the problem to be "grappled with" was one of "overproduction;" and that he had said that we were producing in this country 2,500,000 barrels of crude oil daily whereas, he had claimed, we were consuming only 2,000,-000 barrels daily. I advised him that we had, in fact, no condition of "overproduction," that the states themselves already had the situation well under control and that during the whole year prior to his induction into office our production had averaged only 2,237,000 barrels of crude oil daily whereas we had consumed over 2,559,000 barrels daily. That, I insisted, was not "overproduction," but "underproduction," instead.

Mr. Ickes then asked me this specific question. "What is the authority for your figures?" I replied: "The United States Bureau of Mines, Mr. Secretary —a section of your own department." I then asked the Secretary if he cared to state the source of his statistics and he replied that he had procured them "from the Federal Oil Conservation Board and from the American Petroleum Institute."

And when Mr. Ickes made that statement, he confirmed officially what, in two days, had become my fear—that he was being misled by our opponents.

Why should our Federal Government, I thought, go to the American Petroleum Institute, foundling and mouthpiece of the very biggest of organized big business, for factual information concerning conditions directly involved in a great controversy between such people and the independent, individual citizen whose business life was at stake in competing with monopolistic big business? Free and unhampered competition in oil meant that the "little man businesses" were a thorn in the side of monopolistic price-fixers, importers and production controllers; for free competition, guaranteed by a proper enforcement of our anti-trust laws—themselves born of oil—would destroy such business tactics. I knew that monopoly in oil needed a power even greater than their own to control their independent competitors. And what power, if not that of government itself, was available? Moreover, even governmental power could be enlisted by monopoly only on the showing of concrete evidence that an emergency existed because of the possibility of a violation of some great idealistic principle.

But an issue could be created, even though it

must be bogus. Conservation of natural resources was an ideal readily to be supported by the public. Therefore, shout waste! Current "overproduction!" Future oil shortage! Even the scare about a defenseless nation in time of war! Frighten the public by misrepresenting facts; fool the popular New Deal Administration into acceptance of wrong figures; hold out to a brand new, ambitious and inexperienced officialdom the bait of governmental control of a huge industry—and if anything was needed to usher in for America a New kind of Deal in business, there it was!

Somehow governmental control might be influenced to perpetuate—even enhance—the monopolistic control against which we were fighting!

Let the Petroleum Institute feed Mr. Ickes—and through him, a government official, the American public—the "overproduction" propaganda! Let our government fall hard as a tool to monopolistic schemes. Simply change the real production figure of 2,237,000 to one of 2,500,000—change the real consumption figure of 2,559,000 to one of 2,000,-000, and the issue is alive! Appeal to the vanity of a man admittedly ignorant of the entire matter and persuade that man to start his ambitious march toward the power of "controlling" a great American industry! It seemed to me that our Mr. Ickes

letters from the presidents of major oil companies
. . . concerning the great value and helpfulness of
this Government Oil Board. These men are the biggest on earth insofar as oil is concerned. I can not
use these letters, but . . . you may see them and
know just what these men think and why they think
so."

I knew that for years many oil operators had
been exasperated by the fact that high governmental
officials, particularly the former Secretary of the
Interior, Wilbur, constantly indulged in the practice of making public statements which misrepresented the true factual conditions of the petroleum
industry. Apparently, United States Bureau of
Mines statistics were not being properly analyzed,
or else somebody in the government was supplying
bogus figures which, strangely enough, supported
the false propaganda of monopoly. A fictitious picture of the industry was presented the American
public and it was painted by high sources. Apparently the hand of monopoly actually worked
through the medium of Mr. Rochester, the Conservation Board's Secretary, since that Board contributed false information regarding production and
consumption.

I observed that this Mr. Rochester, who sat by
Mr. Ickes' side, made notes as I quoted statistics

and finally after some whispered remarks to the Secretary, arose and slipped quietly from the room.

I then warned Mr. Ickes that somebody in the government had supplied him with wrong information and urged that he depend upon the highly respected and esteemed United States Bureau of Mines for authentic statistics. The Secretary thereupon announced an adjournment of the hearing to ten o'clock the following morning, stating that in the meantime he would have the figures checked to determine who was correct, he or I.

CHAPTER VI

Meet Mr. Roosevelt

The events which had occurred during the preceding two or three days stimulated much discussion among the group of independent oil men with whom I was identified. We regarded Mr. Ickes as unfriendly to our position and we thought his admitted and demonstrated ignorance of oil matters constituted a grave danger since, through Mr. Ickes, the New Deal would act.

It is significant now to record that of all the governors invited to the Conference, only one, Alf Landon of my home state, was personally present, the remaining governors having commissioned individuals to be present as their representatives. By virtue of the fact that Mr. Landon was the only governor at hand, he, as the ranking member of the Conference, was made Chairman. We all knew Alf as a small oil operator, but we also knew him as one who favored, too many times, we thought, the major companies' view of oil issues. Even then he insisted that the government be given more control over the productive processes of the industry, going so far finally, in a telegram to the New Deal Administration, as to advocate a form of dictatorship for the petroleum industry! (This position was taken, of course, long before Mr. Landon's name even was mentioned as a possible presidential candidate, and later, in campaign battle, Mr. Ickes threw at him the record of his former expressions.)

But we independents, following our first meeting with Mr. Ickes, felt greatly perturbed over the manner in which affairs seemed to be drifting. We met therefore, at the Mayflower Hotel the night of that Tuesday, March 28th, and after full discussion formed the "Independent Petroleum Association Opposed to Monopoly," and banded ourselves together to carry the matter, if necessary, to prominent members of Congress as well as to the President of the United States. All were insistent that everything possible should be done, and quickly, to prevent the new Roosevelt Administration from starting its career with a misunderstanding of oil problems.

We eagerly and hopefully, therefore, awaited Mr. Ickes' expected announcement on the following morning. We thought that he would admit that he had been wrongly advised as to the facts of the oil issue. Such admission would destroy the danger of governmental control of oil production in the interests of monopoly as against the principle of free and competitive enterprise.

The meeting of the next morning was short and sweet. Mr. Ickes, in the presence of our committee and other independents, appeared to be just a little nervous, somewhat irked at the business at hand, and considerably preoccupied with numerous papers that cluttered his desk. After a considerable pause he finally greeted us. His manner was pained, reserved and condescending.

I arose and asked the Secretary whether he had confirmed the correctness of the figures I had quoted on the preceding day. Mr. Ickes answered: "I have had the figures you used checked and they are correct. Figures, however, are subject to interpretation!"

The demeanor of the Secretary, his accentuation and emphasis of his last remark, were so indicative of a mind closed to our purpose that, on his obvious desire to conclude the matter without any further ado—much less an acknowledgment by him that his use of wrong statistics in his Conference invitation had been in error—I, nonplused, answered:

"Well, if the government is desirous of 'interpreting' figures which represent actual facts, it will be privileged, I presume, to interpret them in its own way."

One or two other individuals, including my own Research Director, Mr. Kemnitzer, attempted to discuss more fully the facts in question, but Mr. Ickes showed great belligerency and even anger as he raised his voice, ignoring, in insulting manner, Mr. Kemnitzer, who attempted vainly to speak. Needless to say, the meeting broke up in quick fashion, the disheartened and chagrined oil men wondering what next was to be done.

But Mr. John B. Elliott, Chairman and spokesman of our newly formed "Independent Petroleum Association Opposed to Monopoly," quickly threw himself into action. Through the two California Senators, appointments were made with other Cabinet officers and one also with President Roosevelt. I was one of a committee selected to lay our problem before the President. We did this the following day.

I shall not soon forget the hour and ten minutes at the White House. In his study, Mr. Roosevelt greeted us with great charm and cordiality. I had known him since 1923 and was pleased at his personal word to me as he shook my hand. Chairs had been arranged in a semi-circle about his desk and we seated ourselves at his very hospitable suggestion, in quite informal fashion.

Being in the presence of Franklin D. Roosevelt when he is at his best is something to remember. He has a graciousness of manner that seemingly captivates and influences everybody about him to incline to his view. He, also, very politely and gallantly, agrees with everything that is said. One is impressed, and immeasurably so, with the firm belief that the President not only agrees with, but promises to do everything that is desired. He doesn't "hypnotize;" he doesn't "electrify." His gracious manner, his natural poise, his democratic and social manner of meeting people and of discoursing with them, win the day for Mr. Roosevelt.

The President reclined easily before us, his left elbow on the arm of his chair, his head leaning on his left hand with its long middle-finger stretched alongside and deeply imbedded in his left cheek. He was almost boyish as he asked us to reverse in our minds the ordinary conception that "one teacher usually teaches many pupils." Today, he laughingly declared, he was *the pupil*—we were the teachers. What could we teach him, what did we want and what could the pupil do for us?

Out of the good-natured, intimate atmosphere which the President's personality so easily created, we told him first of the regrettable fact of Mr. Ickes' error in oil statistics. We stated our suspicions concerning the Secretary of the Federal Oil Conservation Board (Mr. E. S. Rochester). We stated the import of the use of wrong information to create a false issue in petroleum. (We did not mention the E. S. Rochester "never-slipped-a-cog" letter to Mr. Creel, although we had caused a copy of that letter to be handed the President on the preceding night).

The President, still in his "pupil" role, most playfully, said, "Well, I don't know who the fellow is, but, since last night, there ain't no Secretary of the Federal Oil Conservation Board and there ain't no Federal Oil Conservation Board neither. That has been abolished."

We presented to him the several recommendations which the "Independent Petroleum Association Opposed to Monopoly" had made as its contribution to the Governors' Oil Conference. He accepted our offering with most kindly and sympathetic gesture. We spent about fifteen minutes in discussing the supply and demand condition of crude oil, I leaving him, at his request, some charts and material which my research department had prepared. We also spent about fifteen minutes in discussing our recommendation for a divorcement of oil pipe-lines from their present major oil company ownership.

Of all our recommendations, each of which we considered to be of major importance, Mr. Roosevelt, strangely enough, seemed intrigued at the pipe-line divorcement suggestion and showed the greatest and most avid interest in our argument regarding the matter. To my surprise, on our concluding the pipe-line presentation, the President, with a rather grandiose, flourishing toss of his head, said, and very seriously, "I think you are right. I am going to recommend it."

As we left the White House, following our long discussion of oil problems, I could not but feel puzzled—almost frightened, at the possibilities I felt might have been revealed by the expression of Mr. Roosevelt and his attitude about the pipe-line divorcement proposal. I championed divorcement of pipe-lines, but only after long and careful study of the effect of their ownership, as constituted, upon price control in the industry and their being used, as I knew to be the case, as an instrumentality of monopoly. But, the divorcement from present ownership of any kind of assets valued at $895,-000,000 (as the pipe-lines were), regardless of the issues involved in any controversy, is a matter of grave moment. Surely decision regarding such a

matter should come only from profound delibera-
tion following most complete analysis of the problems involved. The President had been at his new
job of many and arduous duties for less than four
short weeks. Could he have given great study to
this matter? I knew of no work by any governmental department that had resulted in any conclusions regarding that important subject. Could
the President—and I almost shuddered at the
thought—be so constituted as to pass snap judgment, involving such tremendous considerations,
following only fifteen minutes of discussion of just
one side of the question? I did not then permit myself to go too far in visualising the possible consequences to the nation, were its Chief Executive
so constituted as thus to handle large industrial
matters.

CHAPTER VII

The Genesis of NRA—Its Character

The Governors' Oil Conference of March, 1933, should go down on the record as an important chapter in New Deal history. It lasted for only three days, but it represented the first attempt of a new and inexperienced officialdom to solve an acute industrial problem.

The petroleum industry was the first one tackled by the Roosevelt Administration in an effort to grapple with a real big economic problem. It is my belief that the Governors' Oil Conference first sowed the seed that stirred the New Deal toward the NRA program which followed.

At the time of the Conference, events showed that the President was still "pushing" or promoting that old abstraction dangled before the voters in 1932 simply as the undefined "New Deal." Out of the Conference came ambitious notions that finally bore fruition in the famous codes of industry.

The original motivating force that created this great and novel experiment was supplied not by the young brain trusters—as many believe—but by the so-called "leaders" of the oil industry, in their drive to enlist the aid of the Federal Government in their struggle to monopolize and to control their independent competitors. It was, in fine, the grandest scheme ever attempted to legalize monopoly and to destroy competition. The codes which followed proved that point—and the very first thing done in the scheme was the writing into the Industrial Recovery Act itself, an abrogation of the anti-trust laws, always the great fear of the monopolist! In oil, therefore, the New Deal theory of Federal control of American industry was born, and the oil code, naturally, was the first code of industry to be adopted by the government.

The administration, at the Governors' Oil Conference, had nothing to offer and came forward with no original constructive recommendations. The major oil concerns urged Federal Government control of the production of all crude oil. The independents were primarily concerned with opposing the proposed imposition of such artificial regulation upon the productive processes of industry. Other recommendations collateral to the "control" issue were made, but that was the basic controversy. The significant outcome of the Conference was, I have always believed, the planting of the ambitious idea in the mind of Harold Ickes that he should, in some manner, so play his hand as to place himself in position to "run" the petroleum industry—to be its dictator, in fact.

It seemed to me, also, that the Conference revealed a tendency on the part of the President for grandiose action and hasty and inconsiderate judgment.

On April 3rd, Mr. Roosevelt referred to the governors of seventeen oil states the reports and recommendations of the Main Conference and of the "Independent Petroleum Association Opposed to Monopoly." The President approved of only one recommendation from each of many submitted by those two bodies—selecting from the Conference report that calling for legislation by Congress prohibiting transportation in interstate and foreign commerce of oil produced in violation of state law; and from the recommendations of the independents, he selected and approved the pipe-line divorcement proposal stating that "such legislation should be enacted at as early a date as possible." It is significant to note here that the approval by the President of the monopolist recommendations regarding interstate shipments of oil later was embodied in legislation passed by Congress as the famous Connally Act; that regarding pipe-line divorcement and recommended by the independents, was introduced as a bill by Senator Borah, from Idaho, but never passed, Mr. Ickes advising Congress against it, stating that the President had been "ill-advised" at the time the subject had been presented to him. Repeated efforts of Mr. Borah in this connection have been of no avail and Mr. Roosevelt has not pursued the matter further.

No favorable mention whatsoever was made by the President, in his letter to the governors, of the controversial subject of the Federal control of oil production, although this was the Number One and most important of the recommendations of the major oil company group, which, by the way, was signed by Governor Alf Landon, as Chairman.

There is nothing on the record to indicate that the President, at that time, really entertained a serious notion concerning a centralized governmental regulation and control of the economic elements of industry. As a matter of fact and of record, the President, in his own letter to the Governors, refused to follow the Conference recommendation that he use the power of the Federal Government to regulate development of oil pools, to control production or to force even a temporary shutdown of producing oil wells. He stated, "It is obvious that the action proposed to be taken in these paragraphs is within the sole authority and jurisdiction of the interested States," and that "he might be regarded as infringing on the sovereignty of the States" if he should even make such a "suggestion" to the Governors of the States. Such a categorical statement of position seems strangely in contrast to the sweeping policy of NRA Codes, adopted shortly thereafter, by virtue of which citizens actually were jailed in prosecutions which Mr. Ickes later directed in enforcing the closing in of producing oil wells.

Following the conclusion of the Governors' Oil Conference and the failure of the protagonists of "Federal control" to obtain President Roosevelt's sanction to the plan then presented, a dogged and persistent effort was undertaken by representatives of major organizations toward bringing about some form of Federal control of the oil industry.

Mr. Roosevelt, during the first several weeks at his White House desk, had no thought of exercising Federal control over the productive processes or other economic elements of industry or business, believing genuinely that under the Constitution and the American system of government such exercise of power would be considered an illegal and unwarranted encroachment upon State sovereignty, and, as such, unconstitutional and void. Otherwise, how can one interpret his letter to the Governors, written on April 3rd, 1933, and in which, in commenting on the suggestions and recommendations which had been made by the oil monopolists that the Federal Government should take a hand in regulating the manner of development of oil pools and controlling the production of oil wells in the States, he stated expressly that in such circumstances, "The President of the United States has no (such) authority . . . " and "he might be regarded as infringing on the sovereignty of the States if he should make (even) the suggestion" which was contained in the recommendation.

The historical fact reveals, however, that powerful, albeit quiet, influences were set to work immediately following the Governors' Oil Conference, by the big oil concerns, to put over on the Administration their idea for Federal Control of the oil industry. This idea finally took hold with Mr. Ickes —it appears that the ambitious brain-trusters and young radicals then resident in Washington leaped avidly toward it, and although it originated in the minds of the economic royalists against whom the President himself railed in 1932, the American Nation had the dose handed to them shortly afterward under the sponsorship of the President's "New Deal."

The anomaly of it all seems now to be that the greatest of all ideas which the New Deal seized upon as its *modus operandi* were offered to it by the hated economic royalists whom the presidential candidate had attacked with such great fervor in the campaign. And, shortly, the new administrator of the Petroleum Code was to appoint the captains of the oil industry, the heads of the greatest of all monopolies, to positions on his Administrative Boards and Committees, to rule under an enthronement of admitted ignorance, the entire kingdom of oil, writing the regulations to control the business methods, aye, even the opportunities of the independents, the competitors of monopoly. Under NRA, monopoly was, indeed, entrenched—and in the very substance of the National Government itself!

The press of the country soon carried reports to the effect that Congress was to be asked to pass legislation providing for Federal control. Shortly after, a bill was introduced making the Secretary of the Interior a virtual dictator of the entire industry, insofar as exports, imports, production, etc., were concerned. Secretary Ickes supported and sponsored the proposed legislation, appearing later before Congress and even writing newspaper articles in favor of the plan.

An Ickes propaganda article entitled "The Crisis in Oil: A Huge National Problem," appeared in the Sunday New York *Times* of June 11, 1933, in which despite his having been informed previously to the contrary, he stressed the "waste" scare and referred erroneously to the "enormous quantities of excess production." In spite of the information which had been given Mr. Ickes at the Governors' Conference and his own admission that he had checked the information and had found it to be correct, he, nevertheless, told the public in his *Times* article that "for the present our problem is one of coping with an overproduction which is more serious than perhaps ever before." That statement, of course, was untrue.

I, for quite some time, had published regularly the "J. Edward Jones Monthly Petroleum Statement," in which publication statistical data and comment regarding the fundamental economic factors of supply, demand and price were presented to the industry. When I began to realize that Mr. Ickes was working, along with the oil combine, for national legislation to enforce a Federal control of the petroleum industry, I started, in my publication, to analyze the problem and to oppose, quite forcefully—though, of course, in respectful manner, the lines of policy Mr. Ickes was pursuing. Such an attack on his program was made quite formidable simply by the publication of statistical data, authoritatively adduced, that contradicted flatly and completely the position Mr. Ickes took and the representations he made both to the American public and to various committees of both Houses of Congress as well.

Came the NRA and the Oil Code (now all defunct). Mr. Ickes, the man who, with a bang of his fist in a moment of rising anger, had exclaimed in admitted ignorance, "I am not an oil man and I don't know a damned thing about the oil business," was made Administrator of the Petroleum Code!

Some quality of human nature—not knowledge or intelligent understanding of the "oil business"—suffered Mr. Ickes to accept the job of "running" a great industry concerning which he knew not a "damned thing." But, in life we find that the performance of a novice, is, of course, just exactly like that of a novice. Nothing else is expected. The laws of nature—a Houdini—even a New Deal—can't make a sophisticate of a novice and still retain the novice. Mr. Ickes, as the Petroleum Administrator, never demonstrated anything in his official acts, that belied his first and most authentic statement about oil—that he wasn't "an oil man" and didn't "know a damned thing about the oil business."

I continued my opposition to Mr. Ickes, pointing out his inconsistencies, his errors, his favoritism in the administration of the oil code toward the oil monopoly, until in February, of 1934, I presented to the Members of the Congress of the United States a Memorial regarding problems of the petroleum industry. In my Memorial, I paid high tribute to President Roosevelt and, along with voluminous statistical data pointed out what I regarded as the errors of Mr. Ickes, opposed his policies and made recommendations to the Congress which were directly opposed to the Ickes' program. I appeared before the Committee on Mines and Mining and the Finance Committee, both of the United States Senate, and the Committee on Interstate and Foreign Commerce of the House of Representatives in opposition to legislation sponsored by Mr. Ickes which would have placed even more dictatorial power in his hands than that already lodged there by the Petroleum Code. At such hearings, Ickes appeared, noticing me, but never speaking to me. I steadfastly presented analyses and factual information in opposition to him, although the record will show my position to have been always a respectful one.

I have never sympathized with the publicly expressed views of Mr. Ickes in his blustering opposition to the power of monopoly and "big business." My attitude toward him in this regard has always been prompted by the fact, known to those having intimate knowledge of his acts as Administrator of the Petroleum Code, that when he had the great power of a code dictator, he actually surrounded himself with the heads of the huge oil combines that always opposed the interests of the independents of the industry! On his Planning and Coördination Committee, that important policy determining Committee for Mr. Ickes as the Code Authority, the principal personages on the Committee were the heads and representatives of the nation's largest oil organizations: Standard Oil Company of New York, Standard Oil Company of California, Pure Oil Company, Tide Water Oil Company, Barnsdall Oil Company, Standard Oil Company of New Jersey, etc. There were also a few other men on this Committee: henchmen of monopoly, but little known as independents.

And then, too, I have had little respect for the principle demonstrated by Mr. Ickes when he has attacked "high prices." I knew that under the Code, when he had real power in his hands, his own organization actually fixed prices in the petroleum industry, not at the lowest competitive price of the independent, but at the highest monopolistic price of the major companies. In this connection, I was amazed to learn the benevolent attitude of Mr. Ickes toward monopoly and high prices, when a member of his Petroleum Administration Board, Dr. John W. Frey, in charge of marketing for the Code Authority, Mr. Ickes, testified in September, 1934, at Hearings before the Committee on Interstate and Foreign Commerce of the House of Representatives at Washington, D. C. In that testimony, Congressman Wolverton of New Jersey, by skillful questioning, established the fact that the high price of gasoline was actually fixed by official Washington and that Mr. Ickes' code organization exerted influence to keep the price up to levels desired by the big companies!

Mr. Wolverton asked Dr. Frey whether the big oil companies met the low competitive prices of independent dealers in Camden, New Jersey. (I quote from the *Congressional Record*.)

Mr. Wolverton: Well, did they meet it in Camden?

Dr. Frey: They did not meet it in Camden because I asked them not to.

Mr. Wolverton: Asked who not to?

Dr. Frey: The major companies.

Mr. Wolverton: You mean, you as an official of the Government, asked them not to decrease their price?

Dr. Frey: I did.

Mr. Wolverton: Well, now we are getting down to where the prices are fixed. The gentlemen who preceded you did not know anything about it and I had gathered that somebody was the fixer and that the rest by some means of mental telepathy were able to find it out, but now I find that it is done here in Washington and you are the man who does it, and you are the man who is responsible for what I pay for gasoline in Camden!

Dr. Frey: Not entirely. I have done it in hundreds of cases.

Mr. Wolverton: But the big operators are maintaining prices just the same. Did you ask them not to come down in price?

Dr. Frey: We asked them not to meet that competition.

Mr. Wolverton: That surprises me. I have nothing more to say when I find that the major companies in my locality are charging me what they are at the request of an official in Washington. That is interesting indeed. I do not have anything more to say at this time.

Dr. Frey: We have done that in hundreds of instances.

To give some idea of the manner in which the truth was represented or misrepresented (the reader may take his choice) to the Congress of the United States about exactly what was or what was not done in the matter of price fixing by the government under the direction and responsibility of Mr. Ickes, the following record of the hearings referred to is reproduced:

Mr. Wolverton: Then you would not favor a price-fixing policy?

Secretary Ickes: Not at the present; no. Under the present code we have not attempted to fix prices. We have not up to the present, and I do not think that is the way to approach this problem. We must approach it from a long-range viewpoint.

Mr. Wolverton: Mr. Secretary, if the authority under the code has not fixed the price for gasoline, how does it happen that in many localities there is no difference in price between that charged by one company and that charged by another?

Secretary Ickes: There is no differentiation in price?

Mr. Wolverton: Not in the locality in which I live nor any other in which I have bought gasoline.

I can go to a Standard station, an American, Sun, Purol, Atlantic, or any other, and there is no difference, not as much as one-tenth of a cent in the price.

Secretary Ickes: That may be just a coincidence.

The following is also enlightening:

Mr. Wolverton: I am interested to know how the same price is arrived at unless the code authority has determined it.

Secretary Ickes: We have not had a hand in that.

Having in mind the testimony of the esteemed Secretary of the Interior, Mr. Ickes, the following testimony of his marketing expert before the same committee and in the same hearings, only two days later, is most interesting:

Mr. Wolverton: When the Secretary of the Interior was present I asked him about the question of price-fixing, and he said that he did not believe in it.

Dr. Frey: Yes.

Mr. Wolverton: I would like to know the names of the big companies you requested not to reduce their price.

Dr. Frey: Well, in that particular instance you are talking of, that is, Camden?

Mr. Wolverton: Yes.

Dr. Frey: The Company that was going to cut and I asked not to cut was the Sun.

Mr. Wolverton: When you heard that the Sun was going to cut, you asked them not to do it; is that right?

Dr. Frey: That is right.

Mr. Wolverton: Is that a policy of the board or you as an individual?

Dr. Frey: It is a policy of the board.

And further, a startling negation of the representations of the Interior Secretary, Mr. Ickes, was given as follows:

Mr. Wolverton: I want to know the responsibility for this policy that you speak of, and I want to know whether Secretary Ickes knows that you had pursued the course which you did in this particular instance?

Dr. Frey: I make a report to him every week of what I do.

Mr. Wolverton: Was this in accord with his wishes?

Dr. Frey: If it was not, he did not tell me it was not.

Mr. Wolverton: Did you tell him you had done it?

Dr. Frey: I did.

Mr. Wolverton: Did he disapprove of it?

Dr. Frey: No.

Mr. Wolverton: Then we can assume that the responsibility is with him?

Dr. Frey: I suppose so.

In my fight against the bill which would create Federal control of business in the petroleum industry, I stated in September, 1934, before the Interstate and Foreign Commerce Committee the following, in opposition to the price-fixing of Mr. Ickes' Administration:

"A piece of information, startling in its effect, was that elicited here Thursday of this week when questioning developed a fact that other witnesses had not divulged, to the effect that under such Federal control as is already lodged in the Interior Department, price-fixing by the government itself is resulting. The intelligence, so brought to light, reveals the government made a tool of monopoly in the infliction of a high price upon the consuming public that free competition would reduce and reduce legitimately at profit, no doubt, to the independent marketer. Governmental price-fixing was, in this instance, set not at the lowest, but at the highest price.

"Here is not one case but 'hundreds of cases' in the testimonial words before you here of a government official wherein the matter of monopolistic price-fixing actually has obtained the services of the Petroleum Administrative Board, with the full official knowledge of the Administrator himself, in placing the influence of our Federal Government behind the monopolist in maintaining a higher price of identical quality to the consuming public than that which free competition on the part of the independent marketer legitimately would give. When the Petroleum Administrative Board, wittingly or unwittingly, in its concept of government communicates with major organizations with which it has such close and intimate contact, and, apparently toward which it has such beneficent inclinations, advises that organization, confronted with a healthy independent competition, to maintain its high price level to the consumer while the Board proceeds to use the weight of Federal power and influence against the purpose of the independent to induce that independent to fall in line and to raise his price, that particular governmental agency demonstrates its futility, as a governmental agency, in the performance, yea, even, may I say, in its conception, of a proper governmental function. Such failure, if far extended in our government, spells the failure of government itself in respect to its duty to the public which supports it. It follows the principle, argued here, of Federal control. The adoption by our national legislature of that fallacious notion, born of the vanity of man in a stubborn march to dictatorial power, will not conform to the principles of American government, will not constitute a wise and necessary move as an emergency measure, will not be based upon justifiable facts, and, finally, will be objectionable both to the industry itself and to the public at large.

"America is not yet ready for the institution of doctrines that take the white stripes, and the blue from out the Star Spangled Banner."

Although Mr. Roosevelt had placed the proposed Oil Bill on his "must" list, the Bill eventually failed of passage.

During the summer, I appeared before the National Recovery Review Board, of which the celebrated Clarence Darrow was Chairman. At this hearing, which lasted several days, Mr. Ickes sent a special young lawyer to represent him and a concerted, deliberate attempt was made before Mr. Darrow to damage my reputation in a scurrilous attack upon my personal business.

The attack was not founded upon any justifiable facts and it therefore amounted to nothing. It did serve to prove, however, that the only refutation of my position with respect to the problems of the petroleum industry, was, henceforth, to be a personal attack upon me. Mr. Darrow was incensed at such tactics and warned me that he feared that I would be persecuted by litigation of some kind. He stated that, although he had retired from the practice of law, he would be glad to defend me if I were attacked by the Administration.

In the fall of 1934, Mr. Ickes, the Oil Administrator, addressed a Convention of the American Petroleum Institute at Dallas, Texas. In his speech he dwelt at length in lecturing and chiding oil men for the manner in which they ran their businesses, made great fun of the architecture of filling stations, referred to the "three foci" of iniquity in the oil industry—designating the localities as California (home of my friend Mr. John B. Elliott), East Texas (home of my friend Mr. Jack Blalock) and New York (I live in New York) but not calling anybody's name—and finally threatened nationalization of the petroleum industry!

The American Public recently has been shocked at the action taken by the Mexican Government toward the nationalization of the Mexican Petroleum Industry. Great and adverse criticism of our southern neighbor's action has resulted. The charge of Communism has been leveled at what most political economists would characterize as a distinctly "red" policy. Be it remembered, however, that our own New Deal Administration at Dallas, Texas, in 1934, through the person of Harold L. Ickes, actually made a similar "red" threat toward the American Petroleum Industry almost four years before the Mexican coup was effected.

My studies of Mr. Ickes' connections with and

support of various radical movements and associations in Chicago before his having been called into public notice, warned me against his possible purposes. When he boldly threatened the nationalization of the American Petroleum Industry, therefore, I was not so greatly surprised although I sensed the urgent need of some action toward curbing him.

The radical threat of the esteemed Secretary of the Interior and Administrator of the Petroleum Code, alienated what had been support of Mr. Ickes by major oil concerns in the industry. Oil publications editorially attacked him and he began quickly to lose prestige.

(The New Deal Administration later indicted a large number of the so-called leaders of the industry, many of whom actually had sat on Mr. Ickes' Code Boards and Commissions, which under his direction and rule, had fixed petroleum prices. These self same individuals, now fallen from his benign favor, were indicted, along with their companies, for an alleged conspiracy to fix prices; herded to a selected section of the "Union" to be tried before a selected jury of country folk; and finally purged by conviction in the now famous Madison, Wisconsin, oil trial!)

My mail became heavy with demands that some

step now should be taken to rid the industry of
this man and I accordingly forwarded a number
of editorials together with a letter to the President
on November 24, 1934, in which I set forth reasons
to support a request which I made of Mr. Roosevelt
to remove Ickes as Administrator of the Petroleum
Code. I did this in the following letter:

The President
The White House
Washington, D. C.

My dear Mr. President:

As an American Citizen who has given all of his
fifteen years of business career to operations in the
petroleum industry and to profound and extensive
research studies of the economics of petroleum, I,
with great respect, invite your attention to a matter
which I deem of such seriousness to the welfare of
the country as to require frank discussion of it.

The petroleum industry, as a result of an appointment you have made, since the inception of its Code
in September 1933, has been under the administration of a man, Mr. Harold L. Ickes, who, on his
own admission knew nothing at all about it. He has
surrounded himself with a group of young academicians with no oil experience who seem incapable
of properly assisting him either in the administration of the industry or in a thorough understanding
of its problems.

Mr. Ickes, as Administrator of the Code of Fair Competition for the Petroleum Industry has (in addition to his admissions), by his acts revealed an incapacity for efficient performance of his duties and an utter lack of comprehension of the real issues of the industry that have lost for him the confidence and respect which the industry, under the influence of your own leadership, placed in him as your appointee. I enclose herewith editorial comment from important publications confirmatory of this statement. The editorials enclosed are only a few from many, but they indicate a definite trend of opinion and are taken from oil trade publications such as the "National Petroleum News," the "Oil Weekly," and "Oil and Gas Journal," and from one of our great Metropolitan dailies, the "New York *World-Telegram.*"

Among a great many improper acts and shortcomings of Mr. Ickes, I refer to the following as representing some of those of which I believe you should be informed.

1. Mr. Ickes apparently is imbued with an inordinate ambition for more and more power to dictate the course of the industry's conduct, and in an attempt to influence Congressional legislation designed to confer that power upon him, upon occasion has appeared before Committees of Congress and has misrepresented before such committees important phases of the industry's problems. These misrepresentations have been made by him after his attention had been called to the real facts which

he later obscured so completely and contradicted so flatly by his misstatements of fact that intelligent opinion must conclude his position was deliberately taken for the purpose of deceiving and misleading Congress in an attempt to influence the legislative acts of our National legislature. Such conduct on the part of a member of your own Cabinet cannot be described only as unbecoming a Cabinet officer but should be recognized as a danger to representative government.

Before the Committee on Interstate and Foreign Commerce of the House of Representatives on May 30, 1934, for instance, Mr. Ickes, painted a doleful picture of reckless overproduction and extravagant waste in the petroleum industry which do not exist. His statements when analyzed, convey the clear implication of a production of crude oil in this country much beyond our normal needs and stress the dangers of "waste" resulting from overproduc- situation and, if regarded as true, is particularly Ickes is at variance with the facts of the petroleum tion which he claims prevails. This position of Mr. dangerous because, being represented officially to Congressional agencies it might result in national legislation based upon a false premise. It appears that no person other than the President of the United States is in position to arrest or to curb such practice.

2.   Mr. Ickes has issued false statements to the press of the United States thereby causing the American public to become incited to a feeling of appre-

hension concerning possible danger that might arise from petroleum conditions of supply and demand alleged by Mr. Ickes but which, in reality, were not as he represented them. At the very outset of his career as Secretary of the Interior, for instance, he issued a call for the Governors' Oil Conference in March, 1933, in the invitation for which he stated that the problem of the petroleum industry to be "grappled with" was one of "overproduction." He even cited statistics which were incorrect and when I personally called the matter respectfully to his attention, proving by the U. S. Bureau of Mines that he was wrong and asked that he retract his statement because it raised a false issue, he refused to correct his position and indicated a belligerent attitude of stubbornness in holding to the false position he had created for the Administration. In subsequent public utterances and before official agencies he has, throughout his career as Oil Administrator, persistently maintained a similar false position with respect to the facts of petroleum supply and demand and alleged waste. I am in position to supply you with copies of memoranda issued to the Press and with statistical proof which confirm the statements above made.

3.   By Mr. Ickes' own admission and by his own acts and those of many of his subordinates, he has displayed himself and his administration before the industry, over which he rules, as incompetent, inexperienced, unqualified, temperamentally unfitted, unfair, biased, and as lacking in a proper conception

of real government functions. He exhibits a poor and ridiculous management of the industry's affairs and plays upon public opinion by frightening the people about false issues such as an impending and imminent oil shortage, waste and war—all of which notions are not based upon substantial knowledge of actual conditions of fact. These are factors which have contributed, in material fashion, to the loss of confidence which the industry had in Mr. Ickes as Oil Administrator.

4. Instead of applying himself to the business of learning the basic factors contributing to the real and great problems of the industry and resulting in the controversial issues which so distract it, Mr. Ickes in Don Quixote fashion, "grapples" with false and imaginary issues, small and relatively unimportant to the basic problems, and, by exaggerating the importance of his little notions about the inconsequential matters which apparently absorb his thoughts, makes his administration ridiculous and puerile in its ineffective attempts to aid recovery. The lack of coöperation and respect which characterizes Mr. Ickes' administration is splendidly in evidence currently as represented in the utterances of the leaders of important factions of the industry, by prominent editors who speak the opinion of the industry's rank and file and by prominent State officials who oppose his program.

It is not too much for one to say (certainly it is something concerning which you should be informed) that Mr. Ickes stands today as having lost the confidence of the industry as a whole, and that he is now taking issue with responsible leaders of the industry. In taking that issue he disports himself as a vituperative lecturer, violent and insulting in his language, cheap and shallow in his conceptions of the merit of his opponents, unbending in his attitude, vain in his ambitious demands for more and more power to be given one who has not demonstrated a capacity for the exercise of the power desired. His address made before a convention of oil men in Dallas, Texas, on 14 November, 1934, listened to in silence by thousands and broadcast by radio in which he childishly "poked fun" at the industry and compared the policies of our leading organizations to the prolific antics of guinea pigs along with threatening nationalization of the industry as a public utility is an excellent example of an attitude that bespeaks such lack of comprehension of the industry's problems that intelligent opinion cannot further interest itself in futile efforts to work in coöperative spirit under his direction.

Mr. Ickes' Dallas threat of nationalization of the petroleum industry as a public utility was in poor form and without his province as a high government official since no such development in industry in this country could become possible merely through the frightened whim of an official of the Executive Branch of our government, because of the necessity for Congressional action. His threat, therefore, was unwise and indiscreetly made without any evidence whatsoever of authoritative Congressional approval. It is very questionable whether any such drastic and extreme action would be taken by Congress regarding any of the major industries of our country and such an expression, by an official of Cabinet rank, is almost impertinent in its disregard for proper etiquette toward Congress. This country is not yet under any delusions which permit a dictatorial concept of government of our people.

5.   Mr. Ickes has failed, in a misguided policy, to assist the recovery program by adopting a "shut-in" policy of restricting the production of crude oil to points far below the normal needs for such, thereby creating huge deficiencies in our domestic production which, under his orders, can not legally be supplied by American oil producers but which, on the other hand, can only be supplied exclusively either by a monopoly which draws upon foreign sources of supply through imports and withdrawals from stocks built up from imports, or by producers in this country who are willing to produce in excess of his abnormally low "allowables," thereby becoming outlaws (according to Mr. Ickes), and bootleggers of oil in the supplying of a natural, normal and legitimate demand of our American markets. Such a policy does not "put more men back to work," it keeps them away from work.

6.   Although Mr. Ickes has taken credit for stabilizing price conditions within the industry, his acts have created instability inasmuch as they have enhanced a condition of inequitable relationships

between the fundamental price factors of the industry. Under his administration the marketing branch of the industry has suffered, without alleviation on his part, the greatest, most severe, most destructive and most costly price war ever experienced in its history.

Although before the subcommittee of the House Committee of Interstate and Foreign Commerce, Mr. Ickes denied having any hand in price-fixing, he concealed a fact of startling nature, later brought out by Congressman Wolverton in questioning a subordinate member of Mr. Ickes' own staff, that his administration was and had been guilty in "hundreds of cases" of using the influence and power of his office to fix the price of petroleum products to the consuming public and that that fixed price was fixed by his staff—not at the lowest competitive price of independent operators but at the highest price of dominating major organizations. Such acts of price-fixing on the part of Mr. Ickes' administration have been done deliberately, according to the testimony of a government witness, with the full official knowledge of the Oil Administrator. They have been detrimental to the welfare, not only of the hapless consumer, but also to free and independent competition and to the advantage of major monopolistic organizations.

7. Mr. Ickes, as Oil Administrator, has shown, by avoidance of the issue and by inaction, disrespect of the Presidential recommendation for divorcement of oil-pipe lines from their present ownership,

thereby fostering a harmful monopolistic practice and continuing the existence of a concrete instrumentality of monopoly.

8.   In answering, in his Dallas speech above referred to, charges of failure in his administration of the Petroleum Code, Mr. Ickes admitted failure but excused such failure on the ground that the Code was a faulty mechanism, promulgated without his having been consulted regarding its constitution, and thereby implied direct and adverse criticism of the President of the United States who did actually promulgate the Code. By so construing the Code and its manner of promulgation, Mr. Ickes claimed, in effect, that he now is engaged in a difficult attempt to administer the Nation's third largest industry through faulty and defective Code mechanism. Such admission alone, challenges his availability for Code administration.

Because of the acts and inabilities of Mr. Ickes for his position as Oil Administrator, several instances of which have been recited above and additional supporting data for which can and will be supplied if you desire, and because also of a very strong and wide-spread feeling persisting that he has lost the confidence of the industry which he directs, I most respectfully ask, because of my genuine solicitude for the welfare both of the petroleum industry and of the public, that you remove him from the office of Administrator of the Code for Fair Competition for the Petroleum Industry. The destiny of your administration, of the petroleum industry and of the American public itself, demands it.

With my highest consideration, I am

Most respectfully,

(Signed)   J. EDWARD JONES

The request for Mr. Ickes' removal was given widespread publicity throughout the country, and from the date of my sending the letter to the President, there was set into motion the strangest possible chain of events to affect my destiny that could possibly occur in this so-called free country of ours.

I very promptly received an acknowledgment to my letter from the White House and was advised that the President would give further answer when "the investigation" had been concluded. I still am in doubt as to just what was meant or whether irony was intended in the words "the investigation." Nothing in the White House letter specified the object of "the investigation" or hinted as to who or what was to be investigated.

I do know that whatever in the way of further answer was given to me came not in the form of a letter from the President, but rather in the form of a strangely new kind of "Deal."

CHAPTER VIII

New Deal Policeman

My business operations in New York are conducted from my office at 342 Madison Avenue, the one business address I have had in New York since I arrived from Kansas, in January, 1920, to start my business career. For fifteen years I had devoted my entire business life to selection and purchase in the oil fields of the great Mid-Continent region, of landowners' royalties on the production of oil lands, operated chiefly by the largest of the oil operating companies. I distributed these royalties to a substantial clientele which I personally had built up in the Eastern part of this country and in certain parts of Europe. My New York office was the headquarters of the business which I had established, and from that office, operations were conducted from four of my branch offices—a distributing office in Boston, Massachusetts, as well as one in Dresden, Germany, and field offices in Independence, Kansas and in Tulsa, Oklahoma.

In addition to our regular commercial activities a Research Department was maintained at considerable cost, studies were made and research conducted in the field of petroleum economics, including, of course, the problems of the industry. I personally was intrigued by the interesting phases of petroleum problems and gave considerable time to this work, contributing, as best I could, to enlightenment regarding the too little known elements of it.

Possibly two hundred individuals made up my entire organization—unincorporated, and known as the J. Edward Jones Organization—and it was recognized throughout the country as reputable, successful, expert, and foremost in its particular and special line of business activity.

Although our volume of business was comfortably in the seven figure class and was supported by several thousand clients, we never had been confronted by any complaint on the part of any official of either the Federal or of any State Government. No complaints had been filed against us by any of our clientele and none was pending at the time my request for removal of Mr. Ickes was made on November 24th.

At that time, I enjoyed most cordial relationships with the Securities and Exchange Commission and with the Federal Trade Commission, its predecessor in the administration of the Securities Act of 1933. Immediately following the passage of that Act by Congress, I had gone directly to the Federal Trade Commission to register a "Royalty Trust" which bore my name and which we were regularly distributing to our clientele. I had the pleasure of being congratulated by Mr. Baldwin B. Bane, of the Federal Trade Commission, on having formulated, in 1930, a trust, the provisions and principles of which, so he advised me, met the strict requirements of the New Deal Securities Act of 1933 and earned the exemptions provided for registrations. Mr. Bane told me, that, since my trust earned the exemptions from registration I should not clutter his files by leaving with the Commission the material descriptive of our offerings which I personally carried to his offices, and furthermore advised me to "take it back to New York."

I followed the suggestions made and confirmed in writing my understanding of the exempted privileges earned and of our intention to proceed with our business as theretofore.

I was requested to visit with one of Mr. Bane's aides, to advise him of the fundamental nature of the business which I sponsored and to assist him in the formulation of additional rules and regulations for its conduct. I have in my files today rough drafts of proposed rules and regulations which the Commission forwarded to me along with requests for my recommendations and comment regarding their ideas for regulating the oil royalty business. I gave my views and assisted them in their work.

And when the Securities and Exchange Commission was established, obedient to provisions of the Securities Exchange Act of 1934, that Commission taking over the Securities functioning and considerable of the personnel of the Federal Trade Commission, I continued to collaborate with and to aid Mr. Bane, and his assistants, in their new capacities. In this work, a very cordial and friendly attitude was the rule, always, and I was glad of the opportunity afforded to be of some constructive service.

Within a few days following the dispatch of my Ickes removal request to the President, there walked into my New York office my old friend, Dr. Irving Perrine, a prominent and widely known petroleum geologist of Oklahoma City, Oklahoma, and with him a young man of heavy build and shaggy countenance, whom Dr. Perrine introduced as John L. Flynn, a lawyer newly on the staff of the Securities and Exchange Commission. I knew that Dr. Perrine had joined the staff of the Commission as their expert advisor on oil matters and he informed me that he, with Mr. Flynn, were desirous of "getting acquainted" with the oil royalty men by way of harmonizing the efforts of the Commission in the direction of the regulation of their businesses as a branch of the Securities business, and that he had felt pleasure in bringing Mr. Flynn first to me, as, so he stated, I was recognized as heading the foremost organization in the business under survey.

I was, of course, pleased at the call and, after an exchange of the usual courtesies, offered the facilities of myself and my organization toward any good purpose, stating my admiration for the principles which prompted Congress in the establishment of the Commission and making some brief comment concerning what I regarded as a real need for some such agency of government.

Dr. Perrine thanked me in polite and familiar manner and proceeded to outline some of his views regarding the good results he expected to accomplish for the government by virtue of his wide acquaintanceship among oil men. He stood actually aghast, a few seconds later however, and I was seized with complete amazement, when young Mr. Flynn, in most impolite, hostile and even menacing manner, launched into a series of swift and curt questions which he directed at me regarding most intimate details of my own business methods, particularly as to our cost and sale prices, my profits, etc. Dr. Perrine stood this sort of thing for a few minutes, whereupon he informed me, as he frowned upon Mr. Flynn, that he had been sent to New York to interview people, and that Mr. Flynn had simply accompanied him. Also, that on coming into my office, he had not intended any such examination as Mr. Flynn had started, that he thought the tactics were impolite and improper, that he was sorry for the incident and that it had interrupted his conversation with me and his plans—for which he was regretful.

The two gentlemen then departed, having invited me to come to Washington to meet with some additional new personnel of the Commission for the purpose of discussing with such personnel means by which the purposes of the Commission in the regulating of the Royalty Business could best be attained. We set a date for such meeting within a few days following.

When I arrived at the offices of the Commission in Washington, I felt no longer the ease of congenial atmosphere which always previously had characterized the place. I was received with an air of formality (a girl secretary or receptionist directing me to an outsideish-like small office, where I sat on a hard bench for a seemingly interminably long period). Finally, I was ushered through a door and a passage into a small room which, on entering, I perceived to be fairly well filled with personages who somewhat stiffly acknowledged my introduction to them.

Dr. Perrine was present as was also the Mr. Flynn who had visited me in New York. Among others, I met Commissioner Landis, of the Commission, and a Mr. John J. Burns, General Counsel of the Commission, who sat, authoritatively, at the big desk, centered in the room and surrounded by chairs which the others present occupied.

I had not understood that the meeting was to be of the nature of a formal hearing, but, nevertheless, a court stenographer was called and an atmosphere that should have been lightened by so many bright young faces present, became stilted with enforced formality as Mr. Burns, a young Irishman with a decided Harvard accent began to speak for the benefit of the record!

At the outset of his remarks, Mr. Burns alleviated, in some small degree, the tension which I had begun to feel at the stiff and unnatural setting that had been provided. He stated that he wanted me to understand that it was now the practice of the Commission to make a record of all conferences but that the Commission had no complaint whatsoever against me and was not holding the meeting for any such purpose. On the other hand, Mr. Burns complimented me by advising me that the Commission regarded me as heading the "premier organization" of its kind, and they wanted to solicit my coöperation to aid the Commission in what they all recognized as a difficult problem in the regulation of the business which I sponsored, since such business was somewhat technical in nature. He stated that the Commission could benefit if it could have the assistance and coöperation of myself and my entire organization.

Mr. Burns, explaining the necessity for his immediate departure, thereupon arose and left the room. On his leaving, Mr. Flynn, who had sat perfectly quiet but watching me closely, immediately took Mr. Burns' seat at the desk and, once again, without even any polite deference to the thoughts just expressed by Mr. Burns, began a vigorous and obviously hostile, almost brutal style of questioning which plainly indicated an antagonism toward me and my business. He drove hard at field costs, stressed the urgent need to be supplied with information regarding my profits in my business, demanded, in the court-room style of a prosecuting attorney of some homicide bureau, to be informed as to my abilities to assess values of oil properties, insisted upon being supplied, and in quick order, with the names and addresses of my clients and, in general, opened what an up-to-date Chinaman might have regarded as hostilities in an undeclared war.

Dr. Perrine arose and protested the treatment to which I was being subjected. He stated that I was an individual of wide experience in oil field buying, that I was a man of reputation so far as my abilities to judge oil property values was concerned, that he objected to a line of questioning about the profits which were made in business, and that, as he considered it an honor to know me and my organization, he would be embarrassed to remain any longer in the room. Dr. Perrine thereupon strode from the room. I promised to supply Mr. Flynn with the information he desired and the meeting was concluded.

On returning to my New York office, I started the work of accumulating the data demanded by Mr. Flynn and notified the Commission that the material would be forwarded at the earliest possible moment. My extreme bewilderment, therefore, can be imagined when, only a few days before Christmas, I received a telegraphic notice from the General Counsel of the Commission, the young Mr.

Burns, summoning me to be present at a hearing to be held at the New York office of the Commission on December 26th, the day after Christmas, for the announced purpose of conducting an investigation into my personal business activities!

CHAPTER IX

Let the Seller Beware!

The wrath of the American Government on the warpath against any particular individual, is something with which to cope. When orders "to get a man" originate at the top and go down the line through all the cogs of governmental machinery, there is a force, a power, an influence let loose that almost baffles opposition. The only thing that can successfully withstand it is the might of truth, ably and, of course, expensively presented, and supported by those fundamental principles of the American Governmental system which still stand as mighty bulwarks against tyrannical abuses of power to the detriment of individual freedom in this country.

If there is any great weakness in the American Democracy, such lies in the idealism of it. For constitutional government in this country is built upon principles of honor, sometimes to be subverted by the acts of man.

The acts of government which fall in any category other than that of honor are not the legitimate acts of American Government but rather those of "little men dressed in brief authority" who, by some quirk of fate, find themselves within the governmental machinery and clothed with a power they know not how to wield. And such acts eventually will run afoul of those protective provisions of our government which guarantee to us, in the end, that freedom which makes us admire the principles, respect the majesty and love with patriotic fervor the justice of our government.

And just so far as our government is a government of laws, based upon the highest principles of honor written in the Charter of our very existence, the Constitution of the United States, to that exact degree it is *not* a government of men, whose acts may be motivated by all the influences, great and small, that sway human emotions and prejudices.

The long two and one-half years of struggle for everything I hold dear in this world, into which I was thrown by the action announced by the telegram I received from the Securities and Exchange Commission, was a struggle, proved by the record, not against the legitimate acts of my government, not in violation of any of the valid laws of the land, but against the unwise acts of unwise officialdom, an officialdom which, in the celebrated words of the Supreme Court of the United States in its decision later handed down in my own case found "no support in right principle, or in law. It is wholly unreasonable and arbitrary. It violates the cardinal precept upon which the Constitutional safeguards of personal liberty ultimately rest—that this shall be a government of law—because to the precise extent that the mere will of an official or an official body is permitted to take the place of allowable official discretion or to supplant the standing law as a rule of human conduct, the Government ceases to be one of law and becomes an autocracy."

Knowing that I ever had been zealous in directing my business, to the best of my ability, along scrupulous lines of conduct with due regard always to every legal requirement, having in mind my oft-reiterated expressions of willingness to abide by whatever rules the Commission might make with regard to my business, recalling my pleasant relationship with the Commission and their complimentary attitude and their assurances to me, I was greatly puzzled at the definitely hostile attitude of their new lawyer, Flynn, as well as the launching of the investigation of my business activities. I telephoned Mr. Burns, the general counsel, in an effort to learn the reasons for the obvious shift in the Commission's attitude, but met with a cold, non-committal, and hostile reception that did me no good.

I realized that somebody in the government was determined to cause the machinery of government to be turned against me, although, at first, I could not sense the real source of my trouble. I hired legal services, spent a miserable Christmas in trying to conceal my worry and anxiety from my family and my friends, and awaited the morning of the 26th with puzzled concern.

The hearing that started; its method of conduct; the indignities to which I was subjected, in spite of my rights as a citizen; and the knowledge gained as to the high source of origination of the case which had been launched—all contributed, along with the sequence of events that followed, to a long and bitter struggle for my individual freedom, my liberty, my very existence! Eventual victory for me—costly beyond a measure never to be realized—came in two great legal actions: one culminating in a final decision of the United States Supreme Court and one ending in the final verdict of a jury of twelve men of my peers. In the Supreme Court's own words, my victory proves that in America "arbitrary power and the rule of the Constitution cannot both exist. They are antagonistic and incompatible forces; and one or the other must of necessity perish whenever they are brought into conflict." That ruling alone is so basically important to the safeguarding of freedom for individual citizens as against the tyrannical acts and despotic power of usurpers in government in this country, that the sacrifice made is willingly laid down.

Arriving at the offices of the Commission at 120 Broadway, with my counsel, Mr. George S. Leisure, I found the Commission represented in its action against me by their new lawyer, the hostile, young Mr. Flynn, supported by a staff of assistants.

I was informed by another lawyer of the Commission's staff, who acted as the judge, or trial examiner, that the investigation was to be conducted by authority of an "order" of the Securities and Exchange Commission. At the very outset I asked to be apprised of the nature of the complaint which I was advised, for the first time, the Commission had against me.

Strange as it may seem, the Securities and Exchange Commission insisted upon conducting its investigation of me, but refused to advise me of the nature of its complaint, if any of such it had. I desired to know, of course, what it was I should defend myself against and I therefore said: "This being the first time that I have heard from the Commission that there was any complaint whatsoever lodged against any of my operations, I do not know whether I am within my rights to ask the nature of the complaint . . . I am not aware of any complaint. I do not know the nature of it. I would ask you to let me know what that is. . . . I appear to have been summoned here to give you information, and I would think—my instinct would tell me, at least, that I should be apprised of the nature of the complaint."

But the trial examiner advised me that he himself didn't know what the complaint was! He said, "As to the nature of that complaint, I am not advised. I do not know what the information is!"

I then asked, "What is the nature of the violation alleged or otherwise?" The trial examiner answered, "That I am not informed of, other than what is stated in the order. I would not be informed as the Trial Examiner!"

I therefore was compelled to subject myself to a searching, brutal and hostile investigation of many complicated aspects of my private and personal business affairs without knowing of any charge against me except that the Commission had "ordered" the investigation. The Supreme Court later, in my own case, condemned "fishing expeditions" and the Commission, saying: "The Citizen when interrogated about his private affairs, has a right before answering to know why the inquiry is made; and if the purpose disclosed is not a legitimate one he may not be compelled to answer." The Court further stated that, "An investigation not based upon specified grounds is quite as objectionable as a search warrant not based upon specific statements of fact. Such an investigation or such a search, is unlawful in its inception."

I was handed, at this first appearance before the trial examiner, a subpoena requiring the production by me of voluminous books, files and records, among which particularly was demanded the names and addresses of my clients.

I knew of no reason why I should not make such records available to the Commission and I thereupon agreed to a stipulation which permitted the Commission "to examine" such records "at" my office for my "convenience" (in not being compelled to bring such voluminous material to the offices of the Commission). The stipulation, which was signed by counsel of both parties, specifically stated the examination of my books and records was to take place "at" my office—no provision at all being incorporated for their removal.

There followed an examination at my offices of books and records, such examination being conducted by one William H. Rabell, Assistant Chief Investigating Accountant for the Commission, under the immediate and personal direction of Flynn. Five or six accountants worked in my offices under Rabell's direction, the entire procedure, of course, completely demoralizing and disorganizing my own office staff, and disrupting my business operations as well.

The names and addresses of my clientele were obtained by Flynn and the destruction of my standing in my business started in as deliberate an attempt to destroy and to ruin as possibly could be put into motion. Telegrams were sent promiscuously to a satisfied clientele to shock, to warn, to shatter confidence. The following words, telegraphed to my uncomplaining clients, was their first notice that something was wrong:

"Please arrange to be at office of the Securities and Exchange Commission One Twenty Broadway Room Nineteen Eleven New York City at your earliest convenience this afternoon or tomorrow and bring with you all your correspondence literature and records relative to your purchase of royalty trust certificates from J. Edward Jones.

Securities and Exchange Commission

By John L. Flynn."

Interviews with the clients followed, at which Flynn made insinuations and categorical statements to create apprehension concerning the safety of the investments which had been made with me. He even dictated his own version of complaints he wished to be made, following his talks with my clientele, submitting such to the clients in an endeavor to have the complaints signed. Refusal to sign such dictated complaints was given by several of my clients, but others, influenced as they were by an officer of the government, and frightened, of course, signed as directed.

Some of my clients who signed the complaints dictated by Flynn, later came to me and told me they had signed such affidavits because Flynn had frightened them concerning the soundness of their investments and had told them that if they would sign the complaints he would have their money returned to them. Numerous statements along this line were made to me and I possess evidence to that effect.

A particularly insidious situation which seemed deliberately designed to take from me the business which, through long years of effort, I had established as my own, developed almost immediately on the taking from my office of the confidential list of my valued clientele. Those clients thereupon began to be solicited by at least three concerns, of new and unknown standing, who set themselves up as my "competitors."

I have affidavits from clients, who, on interviewing one concern which, in some manner, became possessed of the names of my clients, were advised by the head of that concern, one Mr. Bush (who later was put into jail by the Attorney General of the State of New York) that the Securities and Exchange Commission had "pulled a van" up to my office door and had taken all my books and records from me. He slandered me and my business, referring constantly to the Commission's action against me, and finally telephoned one Osterweil, of the Securities Commission's staff, with whom he conversed on most cordial basis and to whom he addressed a letter of introduction, which he gave to the clients who were present, asking them to go down to the Commission and to file a complaint against me. I have evidence of this matter, including photostatic copies of the letters of introduction given. I was later advised, and by a member of the Commission's own staff (as will be revealed herein), that Osterweil passed out the names and addresses of my valued clients to persons who thereupon circularized them for attempted sales of other offerings.

The examination continued "at" my office in accordance with the written stipulation until on Saturday, January 5, 1935. On this day, at about 2:30 in the afternoon, I returned to my office from luncheon, to find strange men, under the direction of Rabell, carrying armloads of my books and records, including files of correspondence, from my office.

With indignation and emphasis, I protested this action to Rabell, calling his attention to the provisions of the stipulation to the effect that the examination was to be conducted "at" my office and stating that I objected to the seizure and removal of my records, insisting that such action constituted violations of my constitutional rights. My objections, however, met with an attitude of scorn on the part of Rabell, who scoffed at my statements, threatened me with arrest in case I interfered with "Federal men," and refused to cease the seizure and removal of my books, papers and files.

These records were taken to the Commission's offices at 120 Broadway, later indeed, to be removed to Washington, D. C., and not to be returned to my offices until the following March 11th.

The hearings at the Commission's offices continued throughout the greater part of the month of January. I spent many days in giving testimony, confronted by an irate and bellicose Mr. Flynn, who, at all times, employed a brutal method, questioning me as if I were a convicted horse thief.

As this thing proceeded I was naturally very much perturbed and distracted. I could not understand why "the investigation" should have been directed against me and I accordingly dispatched to Washington, one of my counsel, a gentleman of eminent standing, and one of my regular office staff, a man who, prior to his coming with my organization, had done duty in the intelligence service of the State Department. I instructed both of the gentlemen to ascertain, if possible, the reason for the attack against me.

To my great amazement, I was advised that Mr. Ickes, following my request to the President for his removal, had instructed the head of the Secret Service of the Interior Department, one Mr. Glavis, to obtain information concerning my business activities and to supply such to the Securities and Exchange Commission. I learned, from the same source, that Mr. Glavis had communicated with a Mr. Montgomery, then with the Commission, concerning certain information about our operations which Glavis had obtained through the tapping of the telephone wires of my New York office!

And, what hurt me more, I was advised—authoritatively, from an unimpeachable source—(later, indeed to be confirmed in a statement by a member of the Securities and Exchange Commission's staff—as will be noted herein) that a member of the Presidential Secretariat had gone from the White House to the Securities and Exchange Commission with the request that the Commission "get a case" on me and that it "make it a cinch!"

Young Mr. Flynn, the new legal addition to the Commission's talent was, I also learned, the nephew of Mr. Ed Flynn, Democratic leader of New York City's great Bronx and probably the President's closest political friend and confidante. Mr. Flynn was assigned to the Commission and his very first job was the "J. Edward Jones Case."

The Hon. Bainbridge Colby, former Secretary of State under President Wilson, and an old acquaintance of mine, went before the Commission at Washington in my behalf, and obtained from Mr. Burns, the General Counsel, an oral stipulation and agreement that for and in consideration of my going before the Commission and coöperating, I would be given the privilege, following the conclusion of the presentation by Mr. Flynn, of presenting refutation in my own defense. I, therefore, even in the face of the forcible seizure of my books and records, continued with the hearings which did not conclude with Flynn's presentation until January 23rd, 1935.

In spite of the agreement had with my counsel, Mr. Colby, and although I had proceeded in the understanding arrived at by him with the General Counsel, the Commission refused to permit of sufficient time for the presentation by me of my side of the case, or to call witnesses in my behalf. The Commission, on a Saturday afternoon, with rain pouring, suddenly closed its side of the case without any warning having been given prior to that day, and, in such circumstances, catching us, of course, without any witnesses present.

My counsel for the hearing, Mr. George S. Leisure, asked for time to call a few witnesses—petroleum engineers—to testify regarding values of oil properties in Oklahoma. The hearing however, was adjourned, subject to call at the will of the Commission, which never reopened it again. The official stenographer recorded the following: "Whereupon, on January 23, 1935, at 3:20 P.M., the hearing was adjourned subject to further notice of resumption." And to this day no further notice has been given of any resumption of the hearings thus closed.

Throughout the hearing, on numerous occasions, as the record will show, the trial examiner repeatedly promised me opportunity to bring out certain facts on "cross-examination." The record also shows however, that although I had fully complied with their wishes, I was refused that opportunity.

In addition to the fact that the Commission, in spite of their agreement with Mr. Bainbridge Colby and the promises made on the record by the trial examiner himself, denied me the privilege of presenting my defense and to refute the allegations made, a thing was done in the conduct of the investigation of my books and records that, because of subsequent happenings, is worthy of special mention.

In the words of Rabell himself, later to be quoted in a following chapter concerning a most extraordinary episode, Flynn ordered Rabell to "chop off" my books at a certain date, December 27, before final entries had been made by my Auditing Department, and to ignore information at hand in my files, in order to "frame" a case against me by charging an untrue state of affairs in my business.

Following the conclusion of the formal hearings by the Commission, on January 23rd, Flynn and Rabell, with an assistant by the name of Bouchet, rushed the preparation of a formal affidavit to be used as the basis of a complaint against me. An affidavit was prepared, covering various points which Flynn desired be made, and both Rabell and

Bouchet, as accountants for the Commission, were asked by Flynn to sign it. Bouchet later testified under oath that he refused to sign the affidavit, even in face of urgings by Flynn, who carried the argument to Washington, D. C. Bouchet based his refusal on the stated grounds that he did not believe the affidavit could be proved. Rabell, however, on Bouchet's refusal, swore to and signed the affidavit which had been prepared and Mr. Flynn then and there had his "case!"

The affidavit of Rabell was made a supporting voucher for a complaint which Flynn and the trial examiner—the "Judge"—prepared against me. The General Counsel of the Commission came down to New York from Washington, and proceedings were rushed to file charges against me as soon as possible and before I could think of any defense preparations.

In such circumstances, and on advise of counsel, I consented to a temporary injunction of very strange nature. The injunction did no more than restrain me from acts already forbidden all persons by the laws themselves. It, for instance, forbade using the mails and the facilities of interstate commerce in any scheme to defraud. It forbade, in effect, the selling of any securities in interstate commerce unless there was "in effect a registration statement as to such securities," provided, however, that "such registration statement is required" by the Securities Act.

As I intended to do none of the things outlined in the order, and as I had no opportunity to present a defense at that time, I consented to a temporary order, only to realize that much was to be made of the case by the route of newspaper publicity, and by speeches and "statements" on the part of members of the Commission's staff who felt called upon to make very damaging remarks about me.

For my part, to inform my clientele and the public of the background of the action, I published the following advertisement in prominent New York, Boston and Oklahoma newspapers:

An Open Letter
To My Clientele
and the General Public

During the past year and a half it has fallen to my lot to oppose Secretary Ickes in his oil policy. In this opposition I have memorialized Congress and have appeared before various Congressional Committees in presenting factual information which controverted the position which Ickes sponsored. By such action, I have incurred his animosity.

Although my attitude in the petroleum controversy has been displayed in open and public opposition to the Ickes oil policy—which only recently has been condemned by Supreme Court decision—I lately have been subjected to secret and underhanded practices designed, apparently, to damage my reputation and pursued in a way to cause the ruination of my private business.

In November, 1934, I respectfully asked the President of the United States to remove Ickes as Oil Administrator—citing as reasons, among other things, the misrepresentation of oil facts by Ickes before Congress and to the press in order to induce the passage of oil legislation practically giving dictatorship powers to him for the absolute control of the petroleum industry. I have been advised that Ickes instructed Mr. Glavis, head of the secret service of the Interior Department, to "go out and build up a case against J. Edward Jones." I also have been informed that within one week from the date of my letter to the President the telephone wires to my office in New York as well as to my home in Scarsdale were tapped. Any such low practice I resent with all the emphasis of patriotic citizenship.

Publicity in dozens of papers throughout the United States has been to the effect that Ickes has besought the Securities and Exchange Commission to "turn on the heat" in my personal direction. I am reliably informed he has stated that "I will put J. Edward Jones in cold storage and keep him there till the next Ice Age." I understand that Ickes appealed, through Glavis, to the Securities and

Exchange Commission for action against me.

Following these threats and Ickes' direction to
Glavis, the Securities and Exchange Commission
has instituted an investigation of my business activities. On the flimsy ground of an alleged "complaint"—the nature of which the Commission refused to divulge—I have been subjected, for more
than three weeks, to an exhaustive examination of
the books, records and files of my offices and even
have suffered the indignity of having vital files and
record books taken from my offices. I have been
forced to reveal the names and addresses of my clients, to whom the Commission has sent telegrams
and letters which have grossly reflected upon me
and which tend to shatter the confidence of a substantial clientele built up from fifteen years of honest effort from my present address. I am threatened with all manner of court action and have been
denied an opportunity of putting on the record matters of refutation, explanation or correction.

I have attempted to coöperate both with the
Federal Trade Commission and with the Securities
and Exchange Commission and am willing and desirous of following scrupulously any rules which
they may promulgate. My business operations are
conducted to the best of my ability in that direction. I have had a satisfied clientele, no one of whom
was making complaint to me. If any complaint
or charge against me does exist, I desire to know
what it is so that I can defend myself. All my personal responsibility is behind my business practices.

In the present instance, I have had no opportunity even to learn what "complaint" exists—therefore, no opportunity for defense. I am forced to subject myself, however, to an "Ickes Inquisition" which I feel is deliberately directed toward the destruction of the business which over a period of many years I have built with painstaking care and effort.

Congress created the Securities and Exchange Commission and gave it wide powers for constructive purpose. It seems now to have been made a weapon of a high governmental official for the destruction of an individual who dared oppose that official.

The J. Edward Jones Organization brands such practices as representative of a despotic tyranny dangerously threatening to the very fibre of our governmental structure. The Organization will fight this tyranny in the genuine belief that in its attempts to eradicate an evil from our government it is performing a real public service. It will make this fight in the open regardless of consequences. It believes the best way to fight such underhanded and low practices is to raise the curtain of secrecy from them. Full details of this "grudge" fight will be revealed in subsequent statements in this and in other newspapers.

J. EDWARD JONES

New York   Boston
342 Madison Ave.   50 Congress St.

The injunction order was signed on February 8th, and, even before it finally had been decided upon, Mr. Burns had telephoned the various New York newspapers requesting them to come to the Securities and Exchange Commission offices for an "important statement." Mr. Burns' "statement" grossly reflected upon me and indulged in general representations which had not then and have never since been proved.

The New Deal had started a ball rolling in my direction, but the boomerang, even then, was on the way!

CHAPTER X

Mr. Flynn Goes to Town

Since the date of my letter to the President requesting the removal of Mr. Ickes as Administrator of the Petroleum Code, I had encountered personal opposition on the part of those connected with the Government. This opposition seemed to me a definite personal antagonism, a vindictive spirit of pursuit. At my first and succeeding meetings with young John L. Flynn, for example, I had met with an attitude which, even before I had any knowledge whatsoever that I was to be a formal object of prosecutive purpose, impressed me with the thought that Mr. Flynn felt the urgings of some special commission to "get J. Edward Jones." His bullying tactics in a so-called "fact-finding" investigation that covered the minutest details of my every business activity since 1930, included even the counting of pigs and chickens on a Kentucky farm I had purchased as a home for my father and mother. He went far in the direction of scorn and scoffing—even asking, on the official record, whether I had any pigs or chickens at my offices at 342 Madison Avenue, New York.

Mr. Rabell, who, under Flynn, was in charge of the Commission's accountants at work in my office, paraded before me and my office personnel in impolite and disrespectful manner. His peculiar personal antagonism toward me was climaxed in his bold and arbitrary attitude at the time of the seizure and removal of my records.

And on the day of the consenting to and the signing of the temporary injunction order, Mr. Burns spurned to speak to me when we met.

Mr. Joseph P. Kennedy, Chairman of the Commission, speaking to the press in Chicago, supplemented Mr. Burns' "important statement" to the newspapers of New York, when he felt called upon to refer to the "J. Edward Jones Exposé."

These people of the Securities and Exchange Commission seemed to have a penchant for publicity of a type that would ruin both my business and my personal standing and reputation.

But human nature is revealing. Success in personal effort, no matter what emotions may have propelled such action, is very probable to result in joy and exultation when the goal finally is reached. It is difficult, however, for one to conceive of an ordinary functioning of the machinery of our government resulting in emotional demonstrations of its officials over the discomfiture of an individual, stung and hurt by government attack. Of course we may expect national delirium to sweep officialdom as well as citizenry upon the occasion of the surrender of the enemy's armies, an armistice, or what-not, but for officialdom to "cut loose" on the knockout of an individual citizen is strange stuff, indeed!

But, Mr. Flynn, the special ambassadorial spearhead of the New Deal attack upon me, gave way. He had a big night on that day on which the injunction order was agreed to and signed. He celebrated. He apparently surrendered to a natural proclivity, and how he celebrated!

If anything is needed to reveal the personal feelings behind the scenes in this battle, Mr. Flynn, in his own way, and of his own kind, proceeded to show it.

He had learned that during the hearings I had taken a room at the Biltmore Hotel, across the street from my offices which were, of course, occupied by Rabell and his men. At this room, my attorneys and my special auditors worked on the case as it proceeded.

On the night in question, numerous friends, my

attorneys, auditors, and members of my organization were congregated in the Biltmore quarters, discussing with me the various aspects of the case.

During the course of the evening we were greatly surprised and amused to see none other than Mr. John L. Flynn, legal representative of the Securities and Exchange Commission, come reeling into the room, gloriously drunk, snorting with the strong breath of much liquor, beaming with good nature and friendly to a boundless degree! He staggered directly to me, threw his arms affectionately about my neck, familiarly addressed me as "Ed," slapped me on the back and complimented me on being "such a good fighter!"

Mr. Flynn's diction that evening wasn't as good as it might have been, his enunciation was just a little bad as was also his pronunciation, but what he lacked in his quality of speech was supplied by loud tone and raucous manner. He really held the interest of all those present.

I hospitably asked my new social guest what I could do for him and the answer was a clap on my back and a shout for scotch and soda, "with a little lemon peel, please."

Mr. Flynn has large, fat, stubby fingers, and I shall never forget how, as he drank scotch and soda after scotch and soda, he invariably, between gulps, stuck his finger into the glass and stirred his mixture thoroughly, spinning it round and round with his big pudgy finger, as he passed the evening. As the hours wore on, to the gleeful amusement of my other guests, the Securities and Exchange Commission's celebrating counselor continued his libations to a point where his moods began to change. From the good-natured hilarity of his entrance he slumped into an unfriendly and sullen quietude. Picked up, then, by another libation, Mr. Flynn gloated over what he had done to me, praised himself for his self-recognized abilities, boasted of his previous experience as a prosecuting lawyer for the Bronx Homicide Bureau, and, on further progress, again professed the extreme pleasure he had found in meeting a "good fighter."

Not until the "wee sma' hours" of the morning did Mr. Flynn feel called upon to leave us. Unceremoniously, then, he arose and, like a sea captain striding his deck in a heavy rolling sea, the Protector of the Investor started, in anti-bee-line style, to the door. An associate, Mr. H. Van Cortlandt Fish, who was present, arose, and in gentlemanly manner began to assist Counselor to the door. Solicitous concerning Flynn's welfare, he asked the departing guest not to hurry, whereupon Flynn pushed two very large hands to the chest of Mr. Fish, who is of medium stature, gave a lunging shove and actually sent Mr. Fish somersaulting across the floor plump into the fireplace, which, fortunately, was not ablaze.

With this official demonstration of kind-heartedness, the Securities and Exchange Commission, as there represented, paused only for a bleary eyed survey of everybody present, and passed on out of the room.

The celebration and the gloating, the crude exhibition of personal satisfaction, the boasting, the exultation of a vindictive spirit in the happy feeling of a job of destruction well started, had been demonstrated.

CHAPTER XI

New Deal's "Most Effective Weapon"

The power of the printed word is tremendous. The New Deal Administration, early in its career, rightly appraised the value of publicity and elaborate uses have been made of it to further New Deal purposes.

Herbert Hoover in a discussion of the moral questions in public life involving intellectual honesty in officials and in government, recently asked, "Do you think the government which engages hundreds of paid publicity agents daily and hourly to eulogize its official acts, can hold the faith of the citizen in what his government says? Is it honest or sportsmanlike to answer the argument, protest or appeal of the citizen by smearing him as the enemy of the people?"

One of the members of the Securities and Exchange Commission has stated publicity to be that Commission's "most effective weapon." But publicity designed to ruin the standing and reputation of a citizen, without a fair and public trial on the merits of any controversy between that citizen and his government, is publicity that both imposes upon the freedom of the press and the civil liberties of the individual citizens as well.

Business men of American should realize that it is in the power of highly-placed officials to create publicity by the simple and easy route of the issuance of "press releases," the making of speeches, etc., in a manner to kill absolutely a business or the career of a business man. This can be done without the trouble even of bringing out the truth at a trial on the merits of any particular case. Certainly, officials of the Securities and Exchange Commission have resorted to publicity for what appears as obvious purpose to damage individual citizens in the public esteem, realizing, apparently, the credulity of the people on reading statements of governmental officials quoted in the press.

There really seems to be nothing more authoritative to the lay individual than a press quotation of an official of the Federal Government. Ideas of such an official, by the route of publicity, may become important only because of the authoritative position of the individual who utters them. Deprived of official cognizance, the utterances might go unnoticed as chattering Main Street gossip.

Beveridge, for instance, in his magnificent "The Life of John Marshall," points out that the ideas contained in the great Declaration of Independence were not at all new or original. They had been uttered many times and by many men before they finally were immortalized by Jefferson when he wrote the famous Declaration. Chief Justice Marshall, himself, in as great a legal opinion as history has recorded—that in Marbury vs. Madison, did nothing more than restate that which hundreds of men previously had declared.

Authoritative positions of speakers or writers may lend importance to the subjects treated and disarm the public of suspicions regarding the truthfulness of statements made. This being so, a danger to civil liberty arises when unfair advantage is taken in the making by some official of adverse public reference to reflect upon the business or standing of a particular individual.

An example of what I regard as gross unfairness, is the statement released to the press by Mr. Burns, General Counsel of the Commission, on the day on which the temporary injunction order was consented to. As I have previously stated, the principal newspapers of New York were invited to send reporters to his office for an "important statement." In his statement, he referred to "700% profit" which he claimed I had made in my business operations. He made no mention whatsoever of the fact th$t no such profits had been made by me in my regular business dealings but apparently based his unexplained reference on an instance wherein I had purchased a lease on prospective oil land, which had been absolutely non-productive. When later, the gamble of drilling having been taken, oil was struck, I had naturally made handsome profit. This was perfectly legitimate. It was a lucky strike made in a speculative venture.

Mr. Burns, however, framed his "important statement" in a manner calculated to imply that "700% profit" might be considered the rule in my ordinary business operations. This, of course, was not true. Yet a statement made as a press release, coming, as it did, from the General Counsel of the Federal Securities and Exchange Commission, was news. The publication of it, together with its implied meaning, was, of course, very damaging to my investment business. It naturally created havoc and destruction—as I think it was intended to do. Why, I thought, was it necessary for this "Truth in Securities" representative to imply, subtly, albeit effectively, such damaging untruth? Why should this lawyer try his lawsuit in the newspapers? What decision could the reading public give him, if not, indeed, a "thumbs down" decision on J. Edward Jones and his business? But these young New Deal academicians are, to a degree, bright and smart, and logical deduction of the most elemental nature told me that my destruction was the ultimate end of this new vindictive purpose in our government.

And then, Mr. Joseph P. Kennedy, Chairman of the Commission, close friend of the President and the man who, in the words of a member of the Commission's own staff (later to be quoted in a subsequent chapter) had given orders to "get a case" on J. Edward Jones and to "make it a cinch," proved that he was alive to the very latest developments and availed himself of the facilities of publicity to damage me even further. In Chicago, on the day following my first public brush with his honorable agency, he made reference before press reporters to the "J. Edward Jones Exposé"—whatever that was—without defining the "exposé" or stating what it might be. The word "exposé," however, carried its own obvious implications and it was, *per se,* damaging when used as Kennedy used it.

The Commission's zealous Chairman even went so far as to advise a client of mine, a friend of his (according to the written word of the individual in question), that my office had been closed and that I was "not allowed to sell royalties any more." While exceedingly damaging, of course, to me and to my business, neither of these statements was true, the injunction order to which I had consented having done no such thing. The client, however, alarmed by the advice given, brought legal action against me for a return of the amounts invested with me.

There were other "press releases" and "statements" forthcoming from the Securities and Exchange Commission, all very damaging to me and to my business. It is difficult for me to conceive of any legitimate purpose to be served by such a policy and the conclusion seems inescapable that the New Deal Administration resorts to publicity (quoting again Mr. Hoover's words) to "answer the argument . . . of the citizen by smearing him as an enemy of the people." I do know that neither Mr. Ickes nor any member of his staff ever answered, in open debate, my argument regarding the problems of the petroleum industry.

The weeks following February 8th, 1935, wore on, taking their toll in the form of the ruination of my business and the destruction of my business organization. Mr. Burns continued to inflict damage by writing letters that greatly reflected upon me, attempting apparently, as Kennedy had done, to stir my clients to bring suit against me.

An illustration of what one must recognize as the extreme to which the New Dealers were prepared to go in their program to ruin me, is to be found in Mr. Burns' resorting to the giving of official advice to promote legal actions against me by my clientele. One of my clients had written to the Commission in an attempt to help me. Burns replied, "It is my advice that you should take immediate steps to get your money back from Jones, if you are able."

The client was most favorably inclined toward me and was thoroughly happy with the performance of the investments he had made. He accordingly handed Mr. Burns' letter to me.

On examining the records, we learned that my client's investments—from December, 1930, to August, 1932—had been $21,870.00. By July, 1935, he had received a return of $22,808.67. The advice of the General Counsel of the Securities and Exchange Commission, therefore, for the client to sue me for "the return" of his money was ridiculous —if not, indeed, thoroughly pernicious. Mr. Burns, to give such advice over his signature and on the stationery of the Securities and Exchange Commission, should be presumed to speak with the weight of an authority supported by knowledge of the facts. His advice, however, belied the truth and it therefore follows that he must not have known the facts.

But to give advice of such character without being possessed with knowledge as to facts is to demonstrate irresponsibility! And this, to damage my standing and reputation; to stimulate additional legal trouble for me; to shatter the confidence of my clientele; to bring ruination of my business!

I forwarded copies of Burns' correspondence with my client, along with extracts from the records revealing how shockingly wrong Burns had been, to the United States District Attorney in New York City, calling upon that official for some action to protect me, as a citizen, from such abuse. And I received a letter from the District Attorney advising me that he had forwarded my correspondence to the Securities and Exchange Commission in Washington for action! That, of course, was the last I heard of that one item! That was my protection!

Several weeks passed and the heads of my departments agreed with me that an attempt on my part to register our trust with the Commission might now be received favorably by them. I accordingly went to Washington and sought a conference with my old friend, Baldwin B. Bane, now in charge of Registrations for the Commission.

Mr. Bane refused to see me until he had summoned to the room none other than the lawyer, Mr. William Green, who had acted as trial examiner during my hearings before the Commission and another member of the Commission's staff.

In the presence of these three gentlemen I revealed my purpose. I stated that the injunction order, while restraining me from the committing of no specific act, simply reiterated, in effect, the law itself and also prohibited the sale of securities which were unregistered, "provided they should be registered." I recalled my first efforts to register my trust and my having been informed that the trust had earned exemptions from registration. I wanted bygones, however, to be bygones, and asked whether the difficulties so far experienced in my controversy with the Commission would preclude my registering a new series of my trust.

Mr. Bane assured me, in a most cordial manner, that a new registration by me would not at all be affected by the past controveries—that his registration section of the Commission was an entirely different section from the one that had done battle against me, and urged me to file a registration statement.

I thereupon asked for a form which I might use in filing and was told that the Commission had never prepared any forms suitable for my trusts. Mr. Bane, however, handed me an ordinary investment trust form, telling me to use it as best I could and that if there were any changes required or any deficiencies at all found in the registration statement when completed, we could together "sit down and work it out."

I informed the gentlemen of the Commission of my pleasure on receiving such polite and courteous consideration, assured them of my hope of working constructively with them, took the registration forms they had given me, and departed.

On reaching my New York office, I decided to make application for registration of a Series of my Trust and to submit it to the Securities and Exchange Commission. I concluded that because of the previous controversy it would be wise for me to refrain personally from having anything whatsoever to do with the preparation and filing of such a document. Accordingly, I arranged for such work to be done by a thoroughly competent, able and eminent member of the Oklahoma Bar—an oil lawyer intimately familiar with the business which I sponsored—the Honorable E. J. Lundy, of Tulsa, Oklahoma.

Mr. Lundy, a former state legislator, was widely known as a highly respected, honorable member of his profession, and, on his arrival in New York, I assigned to him the exclusive task of meeting the necessary requirements of the Commission in filing my application for registration. He spent several days in this work, during which time I scrupulously avoided taking the slightest personal part in the business at hand. Finally, on May 4, 1935, Mr. Lundy, acting in my behalf, formally filed with the Commission at Washington, the application which he, as my counsel, had prepared.

When, ordinarily, applications for registrations are filed with the Securities and Exchange Commission, such applications are examined by the Commission staff and if deficiencies in the papers are discovered, the applicants are notified, within ten days of filing, that deficiencies exist and opportunity thereupon is given the applicants to supply, or to make good, such deficiencies. Registrations become effective by law, twenty days following their filing date, provided, of course, that no action has been taken to deny this rule.

Reference may be made at this point to the assurance that previously had been given to me by Mr. Baldwin B. Bane, of the Commission, prior to the filing of my application for registration, to the effect that if any deficiency at all in my papers were discovered by the Commission, I would be given opportunity to "sit down and work it out." Such assurance accompanied Mr. Bane's cordial invitation to me to apply for registration. I therefore proceeded in full confidence that I would be accorded "fair treatment," and that my previous controversy with the Commission would not mitigate at all against such treatment of me.

Mr. Lundy having been given similar assurance, wrote me a letter, after he had performed his service in filing my registration statement, and advised me that I could expect to receive notice from the Commission within ten days of the date of filing if any deficiencies were found to exist, and, if so, I then, in accordance with established custom, would be given opportunity to supply them.

As I have stated, my registration statement was filed with the Commission under date of 4 May, 1935. Following the filing, the days passed and I heard not a word from the Commission. One week passed, the first ten days passed—and no notice, no requests, no intelligence of any sort came from the Washington agency regarding my registration. I then presumed that Mr. Lundy had done a good job and that the Commission and I had good chance to get along well together once again.

I congratulated Mr. Lundy on his accomplishment and awaited, as the days came and went, the expiration of the legal twenty day time limit after which I might proceed with my business registered with the SEC!

The last few days of the time limit soon came and the Commission had not seen fit to notify me of any deficiencies in my registration statement. The nineteenth, or last day before the registration became effective on the twentieth, passed, and I advised my organization, at the close of business on that day, that the Commission had notified me of no requirements whatsoever, and that, therefore, we could, on the morrow proceed with a registered issue.

After my office had closed on the nineteenth day, however, and at a late hour, I received a telegram from the Securities and Exchange Commission at Washington, dated 5:35 P.M., May 23rd. The telegram, sent to me and received after business hours on that day, did not notify me of any deficiencies or of any opportunity to correct or to amend the statement which I had filed. Instead, *my* notification from the "Truth in Securities" Commission was one which stated, in substance, that it "appeared" to the Commission that my registration statement included "untrue statements of material facts" and that it omitted to state "material facts

necessary to make the statements therein not misleading."

The telegram further informed me that the Commission was going to hold an official hearing upon
the matter at its office in Washington, and advised
me that at the time of such hearing I might appear
and "show cause why a stop order should not be
issued suspending the effectiveness" of my registration statement!

A great splurge of publicity was released by the
Securities Commission, of course, and newspapers
carried stories to the effect that J. Edward Jones was
to be called upon the carpet to face a stop order
against his business because he had resorted to what
the Commission felt "appeared" to be "untrue"
and "misleading" statements. Numerous clients
and friends of mine began to look upon me as
though I were some strange, outmoded "curio,"
hopelessly out of step with the smiling and confident
"happy days are here again" complex in Washington.

"Orders" to answer charges about "untrue and
misleading" statements in hearings held by our government for the announced purpose of "stop or-
dering" an investment business, have a bad and destructive effect upon an investment clientele, especially when pains are taken by governmental offi-

cials to create sensational publicity on the subject before even a hearing is held on the merits of the case. My business, consequently, suffered almost total stagnation. Sales representatives began to resign, heads of departments applied themselves to the business of looking for new jobs, and Mr. John G. Scattergood, my executive assistant, a splendid gentleman of admirable character and reputation, actually became quite ill from the worry and distress caused him by the publicity and notoriety which the attacks of the Securities and Exchange Commission attracted to our organization. Sales volume slumped off practically to the vanishing point and my associates advised me that, in face of the Securities Commission's attacks and the attendant adverse publicity which was being fed to the newspapers, all business effort was almost futile.

Having in mind the honest purpose and able effort of the very competent Mr. Lundy, I was very incensed at the fact that the Commission seemingly had resorted to deliberate planning to impute to me improper purpose in preparing the registration statement; and that they intended to give me no opportunity, as was ordinarily permitted, to meet any requirement they might make regarding any deficiency they may have felt had been disclosed. I also resented what I considered cheap tactics in the delay of my notice until the zero hour shown by their telegram—5:35 P.M. of the nineteenth day. The charge of "untrue" and "misleading" statements, too, made so destructive of my business by being used as material for sensational publicity—all this impressed me with the conviction that I was confronted with a powerful, deliberate attempt to give vent to vindictive purpose in wreaking destruction of my business, my standing and a reputation that had been built by fifteen years of hard and honest effort.

Within a few days, I received a subpoena *duces tecum* commanding me again to appear, on June 18th, before Mr. William Green of the Commission's legal staff, at the office of the Commission at Washington, D. C., and to bring with me numerous books and voluminous records relating to my private business—none of which, however, was related to the trust that I was desirous of registering.

It appeared fairly obvious to me that I was being summoned down to the throne of the Commission for a real big publicity stunt—a proceeding which the Supreme Court of the United States later condemned, in a decision in this very case, as a "fishing expedition"—"an undertaking," said the Court, "which uniformly has met with judicial condemnation."

I telegraphed instructions to Mr. Lundy to meet me in Washington and made my own way there, only to meet with a most extraordinary experience with a Commission that, because of its tyrannical abuses of power in an unlawful exercise of discretion, seemed to me to be under the influence of minds wholly succumbed to personal animosities.

The attitude which the Securities and Exchange Commission was to demonstrate at the "affair" which it had ordered, was later to get for it what lawyers have described as the most severe castigation and stinging rebuke ever administered by the Supreme Court of the United States to an agency of the executive branch of our government.

"Arbitrary Power" vs. "Rule of the Constitution"

By arrangement, I met my counsel, Mr. Lundy, in Washington, two days prior to the date of the hearing, in order to have sufficient time to go over the subject matter to be treated. Almost immediately, on his arrival from Oklahoma, Mr. Lundy unfortunately fell ill at his hotel, grew steadily worse to the point where he required the constant attention of a doctor and a nurse and finally, on the day before the hearing, was compelled to inform me of his inability to be present as my counsel on the following day.

I became, naturally, quite worried at the prospect of my being compelled to appear at the Commission's hearing without the presence and services of the counsel who was intimately acquainted with the registration statement which he, himself, had prepared.

In such a state of mind, I received a "tip" on that day which astonished me. A lawyer friend from

148

Boston who found himself in Washington communicated with me to the effect that he had just left Mr. John Burns, General Counsel of the Commission, and that, from what Burns had stated, the hearing scheduled for next day was geared to be a great publicity affair with the newsmen invited. Furthermore, everything already had been arranged for formal action to be taken by the Commission to place a "stop order" against me. I was advised of the absolute futility of any attempt on my part to satisfy those who were to be in charge of the hearing. The entire proceeding was to be a "cut and dried" affair.

As my informant was a man who held my confidence, I became greatly distressed to come to the realization that, here again, the New Deal cards seemed to be stacked against even a fair public hearing for me. My thoughts went, in retrospect, to the "chopping off" of my books as of that previous December 27th prior to the month's-end entries by my bookkeepers; the bullying tactics of Flynn; the forcible seizure and removal of my books and records by Rabell.

"But," I thought, "what about that cordial invitation to register my trust which had been extended to me by Mr. Bane? And his assurances of fair play?"

As I pondered these apparently conflicting thoughts, one thing became increasingly clearer to me. I decided that my attempts toward coöperation with the Commission were not only futile, but also, if continued, most certainly would result in the ruination of my business standing and reputation. I therefore decided to withdraw my application for registration and to abandon my hope of offering my securities to my clientele. I accordingly penned the following letter to the Commission and telephoned to one of my New York counsel, Mr. H. I. Fischbach, instructing him to fly to Washington that evening in order to be present on the morrow to present my withdrawal to the Commission.

Mr. Chairman, Representatives of the Honorable
    Commission:—

I caused to be filed with your honorable selves, under date of 4 May, 1935, an application for the registration of Participation Trust Certificates of the J. Edward Jones Royalty Trust, Series "M". I filed this application in genuine purpose directed toward coöperation with the Commission in its commendable endeavors to secure registrations of important offerings of Securities to the public. I did this, although I previously had understood that the J. Edward Jones Royalty Trust had earned exemptions established by rules and regulations promulgated by the Commission and that therefore registration of the Trust was not required.

In the preparation of the statement which was filed, I procured the valued services of an honorable member of the Bar, one of eminent standing and esteem among a substantial profession and in a noted community, the honorable E. J. Lundy, of Oklahoma. Judge Lundy wrote the indenture creating the Trust, prepared all the statements made in the registration papers in question, consulted with me after their preparation and advised me that they conformed, in general plan, to the Indentures which have created previous series of the J. Edward Jones Royalty Trust. I approved Judge Lundy's work and executed the documents.

Preliminary to these preparations, I had visited your offices here, seeking a *modus operandi* for the registration of my trust. In conference, I was advised, in the presence of the esteemed Chairman here, Mr. Green, that you had no forms applicable to the registration of a Trust similar to mine but that I could employ your regular Investment Trust form (some of which then were handed to me for that purpose) and that I should fill out those forms as best I could, whereupon they would be accepted and, if after study any additional information or data were required by you, I would be given opportunity to supply the deficiencies. I was advised that we could "sit down and work it out."

Although I believe the Commission does, in fact,

notify registrants of deficiencies in filings within
ten or twelve days after filing has been made, and
in view of the conference I had had I expected
to be notified before the expiration of the 20 day
period allowed by law, I was surprised to receive *my*
notification by telegram after business hours on the
nineteenth day, the telegram being dated at 5:35
P.M. of that day.

Instead of being allowed an opportunity, as
others have enjoyed, to "sit down and work it out"
with you, my notification advised me of "untrue
statements of material facts" and of omissions of
"material facts necessary to make the statements
therein not misleading," and peremptorily set a date
at which I might appear before you in formal hearing to "show cause why a stop order should not be
issued" suspending the effectiveness of my registration statement.

I immediately communicated with Judge Lundy,
whereupon close study was made of copies of the
registration papers and to this day neither of us
can discern, by any possible stretch of intelligent
imagination, any untrue or misleading statement
contained therein. Nevertheless, you have seen fit
to issue a press release giving widespread publicity
to such references as "untrue" and "misleading"
statements which, to my mind, places me severely at
damage, in that my Government is, by such release
in effect notifying the public and, of course, my
own clientele, that J. Edward Jones is likely to have
a "stop order" placed against his Trust.

I believe such practice is subversive of honorable intentions in business, damaging to constructive purpose, undermining of the confidence of business men in Governmental attempts at business regulation, and not capable of serving J. Edward Jones well in the circumstances.

I, therefore, with regret and with distressful feelings but with respect toward you, now formally withdraw my application for registration of the Participation Trust Certificates of the J. Edward Jones Royalty Trust, Series "M." I do this because of my fear that the business which I founded fifteen years ago and to which I have dedicated the whole of my business career, will be made the object of continued sabotage.

J. EDWARD JONES

Washington, D. C.
June 18, 1935.

Mr. Fischbach duly arrived in Washington and, after learning from me the developments in the case, approved my plan for the withdrawal of my registration statement. He advised me against appearing personally at the offices of the Commission, stating that he wished me to avoid the publicity that he feared would be staged by the Commission. He advised me, further, that he, as my counsel, could properly withdraw my application for registration, whereupon the entire proceedings, by virtue of such withdrawal, must, perforce, cease.

On Mr. Fischbach's arrival at the hearing on the following morning, he observed the presence of several lawyers representing the Commission, including a very serious Mr. Burns and a very sober Mr. Flynn (my February ninth early morning Biltmore Hotel guest). Strange as it may seem, although the present hearing was in connection with an application for the registration of an entirely new Trust, Mr. Flynn had piled high on a table before him, photostatic copies of my books and private records which Rabell previously had seized and also the transcripts of the previous hearing which, of course, did not even make reference to the trust that I now hoped to register. Present also, were several representatives of the press—ready, apparently by arrangement, to report the details of an anticipated happening.

With such an obvious stage setting, my counsel, following formal opening of the hearing, promptly informed the Commission that he had a statement from me which he desired to read into the record, stating that he believed the statement would very much affect the proceeding under way.

But Mr. Burns immediately objected to the reading of my statement—even before he knew what it was—stating that he suspected "very strongly" that my statement was just a publicity "device" of mine!

The examiner, Mr. Green, before permitting discussion concerning the request that my statement be read into the record, took the document from the hands of my counsel and read it carefully. He then asked my counsel whether he wanted "to insist upon the application to withdraw the registration statement."

On Mr. Fischbach's answer in the affirmative the Examiner asked what appeared to be a surprised Mr. Burns, "What does the Commisison have to say to that?" Burns called for a few minutes time "to confer."

Burns then, taking my statement with him, left the room and went into conference with the Securities and Exchange Commissioners themselves who conveniently were in session in an adjoining room.

Returning, after a short interval, the General Counsel for the Commission advised the examiner that the Commission, after considering the "problem," had determined that "they would not exercise the discretion to permit a withdrawal of the registration statement." He further stated that he would like to state for the record that the Commission would *"refuse to permit a registrant to go right up to the guns of a stop order proceedings* and then seek to avoid it without establishing any sound basis for such avoidance."

Such a statement seemed to confirm our strong suspicions that a stop-order really was the original purpose of the Commission, which now seemed desirous of kicking me out of the hearings into a cauldron of adverse publicity instead of permitting me a graceful exit by way of withdrawal.

My counsel, however, desirous of adverse characterization on the record of a statement which— although scrutinized by the Commission and its lawyers—had not yet even been admitted of record, said: "Before any comment can be properly made on the record as to the soundness of the position taken by the registrant I think the statement ought to be in the record, and I ask permission of the examiner to read it into the record." But Mr. Burns continued to insist that my statement be excluded from the record, suggesting, instead, that it simply be "marked for identification." The examiner, of course, so ruled. My counsel, however, insisted upon stating for the record the fact that I had withdrawn my registration statement.

In consideration of the wide diversity of the views on this point held by the Commission and by Mr. Fischbach, and particularly since the Supreme Court of the United States later upheld the position of my own counsel, the following colloquy which ensued is of interest:

Mr. Fischbach: As counsel for J. Edward Jones, the registrant, I wish to note on the record the formal withdrawal by the registrant of—

Examiner Green: You mean request for withdrawal, do you not?

Mr. Fischbach: Well, I mean, Mr. Examiner, exactly what I said.

Examiner Green: You recognize, of course, that you have no power or authority to withdraw a registration statement without the consent of the Commission.

Mr. Fischbach: Our minds do not meet on the subject, Mr. Examiner, and I wish to note on the record the formal withdrawal by the registrant of the registration statement signed by the registrant and filed under date of the 4th of May, 1935, with the Securities and Exchange Commission, identified with this proceeding as file No. 2-1408, and I wish to state with respect to the withdrawal of such registration statement that there is no proceeding before the Examiner.

Examiner Green: With regard to the application of the registrant to withdraw his registration statement, I direct his attention to rule 47 of the Commission which provides, among other things:

'Any registration statement or amendment thereto may be withdrawn upon the request of the registrant if the Commission consents thereto.'

In view of the rule and regulation of the Commission, and the action of the Commission heretofore taken on your application for withdrawal, I will not permit a withdrawal, and we will proceed.

Mr. Fischbach: May it be noted of record that further proceedings to be had based on the registration statement, it is not my intention nor the intention of my associate, Mr. Toomey, to participate in any of the proceedings and that we wish the record to show formally that although we may be present at some part of the proceeding, that our presence is that of spectators.

Examiner Green: Has the Commission anything to say?

Mr. Burns: In view of the ruling of the Examiner I think comment is unnecessary.

Examiner Green: Very well. The record will show that Mr. Jones is not now appearing by counsel.

The hearing was adjourned until June 27th. While it proceeded, however, and before such adjournment, I sought relaxation by visiting Washington's very splendid zoo.

I, for some time, had wanted to see the zoo, particularly because of the fact that considerable publicity had appeared in Washington newspapers regarding some interesting construction work done there under the direction of Mr. Harold Loy Ickes with public funds supplied him by Congress. I had been intrigued by the story, then being narrated in Washington, to the effect that the esteemed Interior Secretary had accomplished what in those times seemed to be an admirable three-fold purpose: spending public money, putting men to work and doing a charitable thing for the mountain goats, herded within the confines of the capital city's zoo.

As the story ran, it seemed that there were no mountains in Washington's zoo and that the mountain goats resident in that urban center were without their natural habitat. No record existed of any protest of intelligence on the part of the mountain goats but story again had it that sympahy had been created in the minds of some of the economic radicals of the New Deal whose brain-trusting was being expanded to great limits in devising schemes of all sorts which might hold promise for the spending of large sums of the people's money. But enough of that—the people are not the goats, and the Washington goats, being of the mountain variety, must have their mountains somehow!

Should Mr. Ickes move a mountain and thereby bring to the Zoo Goats a New Deal to prisoners? No—but Mr. Ickes would "figure out" some answer to the perplexing problem. And Mr. Ickes did so "figure." He decided to *create* a mountain.

Accordingly engineers, architects, brain-trusters, contractors, professors, laborers, treasury check writers—men of many trades were "put back to work" to build a mountain in Washington's zoo down by the corner of the place where the poor mountain goats were wont to herd on the cruel levels of the rockless terrain.

Out of this purpose there grew to fruition a huge strange something that the disrespectful habitually referred to as the "Ickes Monstrosity" but which reasonable human intelligence was supposed to conclude was a perfectly good mountainous crag, wild and real enough to appeal strongly to the natural instincts of animals other than humans.

On completion of this New Deal fantasy, the humans who had built it slipped quietly away from the place, while the mountain goats were driven back to it from other parts of the zoo whither they had gone during construction. But the goats exhibited great alarm and, in fear, fled the scene, exhibiting little gratitude for the present which hard earned public dollars had bought for them. All of the herd, without exception, remained constantly as far away from their New Deal home as high fences would permit.

Finally, the guide who showed me the place said, Mr. Ickes ordered some of his helpers to corner and to seize one of the goats and to take him, forcibly, to the top of the new "mountain" so that, by presence enforced, the goat might become acclimated to the new whatever-the-goat-might-call-it. This was done by the regularly employed of Mr. Ickes' staff, and when the goat's legs actually were freed on top of the ragged "cliff" which had been constructed, the poor thing, instead of bleating its grateful thanks to the great White Father, sprang in terrified and fearful manner from the very highest point straight away to the hard ground below, breaking two of its legs and necessitating its "liquidation" by the merciful guns of Uncle Sam.

Such was the story, and my visit to the scene of the experiment, which, by the way, was then devoid of goats, would have provided pleasant relaxation except for my reflections, compelled by the ludicrous sight, which were concerned with who finally might become the real goats for all the great experiments now under way by virtue of the new directing of things from Washington. I, myself, at that very moment, in a way, was being given treatment that might be compared, figuratively, to that which had cost the life of that poor citizen of the wilds of Colorado.

I returned to my hotel still in a reflective mood, and, as the day was oppressively hot, on meeting Mr. Fischbach, I engaged a car to drive the distance to New York.

When we reached the city in the early hours of the following morning we were dumbfounded to learn from the morning papers that the Securities Commission again had scored by the use of its "most effective weapon." A publicity release had accomplished another damaging purpose.

Headlines such as "J. Edward Jones eludes U. S. Marshal" screamed a story about how I had managed, in some way or other, to escape being served with a subpoena to be present at the hearing which the Commission had adjourned to the 27th. The news, however, was effective in that it implied that J. Edward Jones was "on the run" much in the fashion of a western hi-jacker, guilty of robbery, murder and other vicious crimes. The mere fact, of course, that a process server was unable to find me after the adjournment of the Commission's hearing was not news of any particular moment. Its being made public, colored with the strong implication that I was eluding the United States Marshal who might have been in mad pursuit, smacked of news involving a thrilling case in which government authorities were chasing a real criminal. The melodramatic nature of such a release made news, of course. Many of my clientele and even numerous of my friends showed strange reactions to this startling news story. Naturally, it was devastating in its effects upon what still remained of my business and caused great pain of embarrassment and worry on the part of myself, my family and members of my business organization.

At the earliest possible moment that morning, I telephoned the New York office of the Securities and Exchange Commission, advising them of my innocence in having escaped, without knowing or realizing it, subpoena service in Washington, and expressing my willingness to accept such service at any time at my New York office. An appointment accordingly was made at an hour on that very day when I could accept service and the subpoena was duly served.

I immediately instructed counsel to proceed, as soon as possible, in bringing legal action against the Commission contesting the validity of their acts and rulings in order to determine whether I had been within my rights in taking the position I had taken, through counsel, at the hearing at which I had attempted to withdraw my registration statement. Inasmuch as I felt that the Commission had exercised tyrannical power in going far afield of its proper legal province in heaping unwarranted abuse upon me, I instructed counsel to follow the action which I proposed to institute, to the highest court, if necessary, in the establishment, once and for all time, of the individual rights that had been denied to me by the Commission.

But an event was to occur in the next few days that was so startling in its revelations, so revolting in its suggestions and implications, that the press of the entire nation carried stories and editorials of a scandal that struck deeply and close to the very roots of the real cause of my trouble.

CHAPTER XIII

"Truth in Securities"

Within the next twenty-four hours, I received a strange telephone call suggesting a most extraordinary step for me to take. The call came unexpectedly and, of course, entirely unsolicitedly, from the wife of William H. Rabell, the Assistant Chief Investigating Accountant who had assisted Flynn in the hearing of the first action brought against me by the Securities and Exchange Commission. It was Rabell who, I felt, deliberately and at Flynn's orders "framed" a case against me and had seized, without any warrant or right, my books, papers and private records and forcibly removed them from my office.

Mrs. Rabell told me it was very important and urgently necessary for me, in my own welfare, to telephone her husband at a Washington address that very evening at five o'clock. She gave me his telephone number and asked me to make the call from some telephone booth outside my office, requesting specifically that I avoid the use of my own office telephones. Mrs. Rabell, in answer to a question as to whether Mr. Rabell had favorable or unfavorable news for me, at once assured me most emphatically that the information I could receive from her husband would be good and very favorable from my point of view.

I accordingly did as requested and at five o'clock heard Rabell's familiar voice at the Washington end of the wire. He forthwith informed me that he had been ordered by his superiors to "pull a lousy trick" on me, that he was sorry to have been compelled to participate in a "dirty persecution," that he desired to make amends for his part in the affair, that he had been forced to "frame" the injunction case against me, that he felt sure it could be beaten, and that if I would "lay $2,500 on the line as a starter" he would show me how I could beat the case which the Commission had built against me. He advised me that he expected to be in New York on the coming Friday, June 21st, and asked permission to telephone me at five o'clock on that day so that an appointment could be made enabling him to go fully into the plans which he had in mind. I, therefore, advised Rabell of my willingness to receive his next call.

I immediately notified counsel of Rabell's approach and was warned to beware of an attempt by members of the Commission's staff to entrap me in a bribery plot. I was advised to have no conversation with the man whatsoever unless a full record was made of every word spoken, else I might face an accusation that could be made difficult for me to disprove.

For some considerable time I had been shadowed steadily and, being greatly annoyed and worried by such tactics, I had employed detectives to watch me and to "shadow the shadowers." My detectives were expert technicians who also were assigned to catch the persons who were responsible for tapping the telephone wires at both my office and at my home in suburban Scarsdale. I accordingly notified these men to be prepared with appropriate apparatus, to record, on quick notice, conversations I might have with Rabell.

True to his promise, Rabell telephoned me on the following Friday, and, as he expressed a desire to see me at once, I made an appointment for him to meet me at my home in Scarsdale at nine o'clock that evening.

I immediately communicated with Mr. Fischbach, asked him to obtain the services of his assistant and two court stenographers and to go with them at once to my home.

My detectives were notified of the impending conference and were instructed to install appropriate apparatus to permit the recording of the conversation both by the two court stenographers and by phonograph recording devices as well.

I made arrangements with the Scarsdale police for the stationing of officers in my home during the course of the evening.

I notified the District Attorney of Westchester County, New York, inviting him or his representative to be present. The District Attorney's office notified the United States Attorney's office and an Assistant United States Attorney came to my home late that night, after the conversations had been concluded.

All the persons communicated with by me performed their respective functions with precision and, along with several of my regular office staff, arrived at my home in good time to install dictaphone and recording equipment sufficient for the job at hand. All records were to be made on the third floor of my home and the conversations were to take place in my den on the first, or ground floor. When I personally arrived at my home at about eight o'clock, I found preparations practically complete, with all the persons involved at their stations in three different rooms on the third floor.

In due course of time Rabell appeared and we went together into my den where we at once became engrossed in the subject matter of his visit.

Rabell immediately referred to the hearings conducted in January at which he had taken such prominent part. He unheistatingly stated, when referring to that case, that "I can lick it."

I asked him "how" and he replied, "Because I have supporting schedules to show it is not so."

To my astonishment, he told me that the government had instructed him to "get a case" on me, and that in his examination of my books at my offices he had rejected evidence and information he had found in the files which, if noted by him, would have negated the case he had "framed" in accordance with his orders. The following quotation from the transcript of our conversation is pertinent to this point as revealing Rabell's method:

Mr. Jones: The Government told you to make a case and you went in and fixed my books and got the things that made the case, as I understand you?

Mr. Rabell: I rejected the supporting evidence which would help you.

Rabell then amazed me as he went on to point out that the real purpose of the Commission in its

battle against me was to work up a criminal case
against me. In this connection the record reveals
the following colloquy concerning the real purpose
of the Commission in holding the Washington hearings and their refusal to permit me to withdraw
my registration statement:

Mr. Rabell: Well, they have another thing now that
    has come up, and that is your registration.

Mr. Jones: I withdrew it, but they wouldn't let
    me, and so I am going to have the courts make
    them let me.

Mr. Rabell: The court will let you do that, I am
    sure.

Mr. Jones: They won't let me. They want to get
    me down there to razz me again.

Mr. Rabell: They want to put you on the pan again.
    All they are working for is to get criminal pro-
    ceedings. That is all they want.

Rabell then informed me that the thing I should
do was to permit him to compile from my books and
records evidence he knew to exist that would refute
the charges which the Commission had made
against me. The record on this score follows:

Mr. Jones: You think that you can go with the
    books I have and take evidence out of them that
    will contradict the Government's evidence?

Mr. Rabell: To offset it.

Mr. Jones: And nullify the Government's case?

Mr. Rabell: The Government won't win this case. I am willing to take a bet. Like I told you over the telephone, I don't want anything out of this case unless you win the case.

Mr. Jones: Well, what is your proposition?

Mr. Rabell: Well, I have got to have some dough. I got to have something for my time. And if I win this case, then I want to be paid. And I think you should be willing to do that.

Mr. Jones: Don't you think that it is a dirty, rotten thing to do when I let you see my books and then they weren't properly analyzed? I know why you are here; but I had very hard feelings against you.

Mr. Rabell: I know it; you hated me.

Mr. Jones: No, I didn't hate you, but it is better for us here to talk things quite frankly, because I think you did as you now say you did—build up a case for the Government.

Mr. Rabell: I certainly did.

Mr. Jones: And now then, d—n it, you tell me that you are going to turn around and build up another case that will kill the Government's. Well, you will destroy the Government's case?

Mr. Rabell: Yes, sure. Because there were things done there that were not right.

Rabell then outlined to me what "investigating accounting" was, and again I was astonished to learn how insidiously the cards of fate are stacked against a citizen when his government is out to "get a case" against him. The following conversation concretely reveals the grave dangers to civil liberties resulting from tyrannical abuses of governmental power lodged in the hands of usurpers who prey upon the public.

Mr. Jones: I can't understand you fellows, how you would come into a man's books through "investigating accounting" and pick out things that you can prove to be violations when there is other information in the same books which, if you took it, would offset it.

Mr. Rabell: That is just exactly what it is.

Mr. Jones: That is crooked business.

Mr. Rabell: No.

Mr. Jones: What is it?

Mr. Rabell: It is just good investigating work.

Mr. Jones: In other words, you have to change my books?

Mr. Rabell: Certainly, and build it up on the other side.

Inasmuch as Rabell had signed the affidavit for the "Truth in Securities" Commission, I desired to learn from him whether he was, in fact, to be a witness against me.

Mr. *Jones*: You will be—however—are you not now in the category of a Government witness and testifying for the Government in this case?

Mr. *Rabell*: Yes, I will testify for the Government, but the testimony—I will give you—I will give you the other side to refute it.

Mr. *Jones*: Offset—

Mr. *Rabell*: Yes, absolutely refute it.

Shortly after the Commission had taken the names and addresses of my many clients from my books I learned from different sources that at least three new royalty firms, unknown to me, had begun to circularize my clientele in solicitations for their business. I was very desirous of learning from Rabell just how the names and addresses of my clients, which, of course, always had been held in the strictest of confidence, could suddenly be obtained by newcomers to the business who boldly set themselves up as my competitors. I therefore asked Rabell this question, "Who gave out the names and addresses of my clients?"

Rabell then told me the name of the man in the offices of the Securities and Exchange Commission at 120 Broadway, New York City, who had released the confidential clientele list to other dealers:

Mr. Rabell: Osterweil is the fellow who gave them out.

Mr. Jones: Did they find out that he did it?

Mr. Rabell: Who, the Commission?

Mr. Jones: Yes.

Mr. Rabell: Yes.

Mr. Jones: They know Osterweil gave those names to Bush? (One of the three new royalty dealers.)

Mr. Rabell: Yes.

Mr. Jones: That is a nice thing to have a man come in and get a man's confidential records, and—

Mr. Rabell: There's another fellow who did it, too.

Mr. Jones: Who is he?

Mr. Rabell: Clark.

Mr. Jones: Of course, if anyone will do that—what do you think I ought to do about it?

Mr. Rabell: I don't think you could do a damned thing!

Rabell then explained to me how he would advise the Government lawyers as to their accounting side of the case, then, "on the side," make known to my own auditors the Government's case and collaborate with my staff to defeat it. He continued to express his confidence in his ability to win my case for me and stated his price as $2,500 cash payment and $25,000 following the successful conclusion of the litigation.

The man who had represented the Federal Securities and Exchange Commission and on behalf of whom that Commission actually issued a public statement commendatory of his record and his character, then left my home, with the understanding that he would return on the morning of the coming Sabbath to receive the first installment of the money he demanded to free me from a case which had its genesis in a deliberate and diabolic plot to bring about my ruination by means, admittedly and now of record, foul to an indescribable degree.

I now had my first records of the statements made by one of the conspirators. When Rabell took his leave, however, I did not realize that a miserable and scandalous situation was to result from the next scheduled meeting with him, on the occasion of which revelations were to be made that were even more despicable and disgraceful than those he had so far related.

CHAPTER XIV

More "Truth in Securities"

On the following day, Saturday, the Assistant United States District Attorney who had come to my home following Rabell's departure on the night before, asked permission of me for two agents of the Department of Justice to inspect and to test the recording apparatus at my home and also for them to be present when Rabell should again visit me on the coming Sunday morning. I granted this, and the Department of Justice agents, therefore, were on hand early the next day, along with all the others who had assisted in the recordings of the Friday night preceding. They gave me definite instructions concerning questions to be asked Rabell and, furthermore, made record of the numbers of the bills which I had obtained for the purpose of presenting to Rabell as the bribe which had been demanded.

Rabell arrived at my home at about ten-thirty Sunday morning, and, on his being received, we again went directly to my den to continue our conversations. We covered a great deal of more or less inconsequential matters, but interspersed throughout our talks were bits of most important information.

Rabell told me, for instance, that the President's Secretary, Mr. Louis McHenry Howe, had communicated with Joseph P. Kennedy, Chairman of the Securities and Exchange Commission and had made inquiry to determine whether the Commission was sure of its case against me. This surprising information confirmed a report which previously had been made to me by an unimpeachable source. The record of the conversation on this particular point follows:

Mr. Rabell: Kennedy used to call me every night, used to call me on the long distance telephone—they are so damned scared all the time that you are going to beat them. No kidding!

Well, I will tell you this much—that when Colby (Mr. Bainbridge Colby) went down there—I don't know who he saw—but I know Howe called up Kennedy and Kennedy called me up and raised hell with me.

Mr. Jones: What about?

Mr. Rabell: He wanted to be absolutely sure that I had this thing cinched.

Mr. Jones: Do you mean the President's Secretary?

Mr. Rabell: Yes.

Mr. Jones: Called Kennedy up and told him that?

Mr. Rabell: Yes, asked him—"Were they sure?"

Mr. Jones: He asked that?

Mr. Rabell: In this business—they were raising the devil down there.

Rabell stated that when he was called as a witness in my case he would "be very dumb" insofar as his testimony was concerned. He explained how Flynn had ordered him to "chop off" my books as of a certain date, thus denying the making of proper entries from records already at hand. He went into great detail as to how he would present information he knew was in my books to refute the points of the government's case. When I asked Rabell to inform me who had directly ordered him to "get a case" on me, he replied as follows:

Mr. Rabell: Flynn said to "get the case."

Mr. Jones: Flynn said to "get the case" and to get it as of the date you could get it. Is that it?

Mr. Rabell: I came to him and said, "Listen, what date do you want to get Jones at?" He said, "Go to this date."

Mr. Jones: Which date?

Mr. Rabell: I don't remember the date now.

Mr. Jones: Well, why did he say that?

Mr. Rabell: Because the books were transcribed that day.

Mr. Jones: In other words, then—

Mr. Rabell: Flynn didn't give you a chance to put your other stuff in there.

Mr. Jones: They didn't give me a chance?

Mr. Rabell: No, they are not going to let you put it in this case unless you do it yourself.

Mr. Jones: Well, in other words, just from the standpoint of moral principles—here, this man Flynn knew that my books could show a situation favorable to me and he told you not to take it?

Mr. Rabell: He didn't give you a chance to do that.

Mr. Jones: He didn't give me a chance.

Mr. Rabell: He didn't give you a chance to put your entries in. He grabbed them off as of a certain day. He made a cut off.

Mr. Jones: That he knew would be unfavorable to me?

Mr. Rabell: Oh, yes; certainly he knew it.

Mr. Jones: And he told you to "make the case" as of that date?

Mr. Rabell: As of that date.

Mr. Jones: Isn't that a —— trick?

Mr. Rabell: And not give you a chance to put your entries in. Every one of your supporting entries that came in before that date, they are not in.

Mr. Jones: They're not?

Mr. Rabell: They were not allowed in.

Mr. Jones: I know.

Mr. Rabell: You got a rotten deal.

Mr. Jones: And Flynn knew that, didn't he?

Mr. Rabell: Certainly.

Mr. Jones: Flynn told you to cut my entries off, and not—

Mr. Rabell: Not to give them recognition.

Mr. Jones: And you did?

Mr. Rabell: I did not take into—

Mr. Jones: Or any other information that was in my office! Listen—isn't that a —— trick, it makes me so mad I don't know what to do!

Mr. Rabell: Holy Gee! you can't help it now. The thing is, to refute it.

Mr. Jones: And those records were on hand at that time?

Mr. Rabell: Absolutely; and those entries were made by your girl at that time.

Mr. Jones: In other words, you wouldn't allow the entries to bring it up to date?

Mr. Rabell: That is correct.

Mr. Jones: Well, that's dirty!

Mr. Rabell: Of course, it is dirty; that is the reason

I am here. Those items were not put in because we were told not to put them in.

Mr. Jones: Will you swear to that?

Mr. Rabell: Absolutely.

Mr. Jones: My God! That will ruin their case!

Mr. Rabell: Of course, that is what I tell you.

Rabell went on to inform me that he had advised Flynn, at the time both of them were in my office in the act of going through my books, that my entries had not all been made at the date on which Flynn ordered my books to be "chopped off," but that Flynn then told Rabell to ignore the information and not to allow the entries to be made.

Mr. Rabell: Flynn didn't want to know. "Those entries," I said, "belong in. He hasn't had a chance to make them. Do I allow them, or don't I allow them." He said, "No, don't mess up the deal now."

Mr. Jones: He said not to allow me to enter them? Here he comes down here and tells you to "build up a case" and you look into my books and you find all the information; you say, "Here, Mr. Flynn, those books, as of this day, are not up to date."

Mr. Rabell: That is right.

Mr. Jones: "All the entries are not in. Shall I— Shall I—"

Mr. Rabell: (interrupting) "allow them?"

Mr. Jones: (interrupting) "allow them?"

Mr. Rabell: "No."

Mr. Jones: He orders you then—he comes and he says, "No, don't allow him to enter them"?

Mr. Rabell: That is right.

Mr. Jones: To "catch his books before they are brought up to date"—

Mr. Rabell: "Before he has a chance to bring them up to date. Catch him right here."

Mr. Jones: "Catch him there."

Mr. Rabell: "Don't take any recognition of them."

Mr. Jones: "And don't recognize them and then we have got a case." Now, isn't that a hot stunt?

Mr. Rabell: Then he had a case.

Mr. Jones: He had a case, but—

Mr. Rabell: You can go into any bank and do the same d—n thing!

Mr. Jones: In other words, when I said in my advertisement that they had gone out to "get a case" on me, I was right.

Mr. Rabell: You were right, you knew you were right.

Mr. Jones: I knew I was right, yes. But—

Mr. Rabell: I don't know what the actual cause of that was.

Mr. Jones: Well, I know that. That started with Ickes—that hard-headed Ickes.

Mr. Rabell: I don't know that.

Mr. Jones: But this is the first time that I ever had it definite that Flynn ordered you to build that case against me and wouldn't permit you to do otherwise. Can you beat it!

Mr. Rabell: Do you see, they had a real case there, that way. But it was not fair, that is not fair; it is not fair to let you take—you should be allowed to put in all of these substantiating entries which would have offset their case.

And so, ran the story that Rabell unfolded of the New Deal "Truth in Securities" Commission's performance. It continued to maudlin details. The conversation finally ended by my giving Rabell the first cash installment of his price to deceive his own government. He accepted the bills, the numbers of which the Department of Justice agents, waiting on the third floor of my home had carefully noted, and started to take his leave.

As we passed from my den into the hall that divides the ground floor of the house, we observed, coming quickly down the stairway from the upper floors, the Department of Justice Agents, my two lawyers, a Scarsdale policeman, my detectives and possibly one or two other individuals. At this sight I stepped into the entrance vestibule of the front door and Rabell immediately dashed across the hall and into the dining room as if he were headed for the rear of the house and to the outdoors by way of the butler's pantry and the kitchen. Confronting him and across his pathway, however, quite by chance, was my butler—a large, genial-natured negro. Rabell, trapped, hesitated one split fraction of a second, turned half-way around, and very quickly began to take from his pocket the bills I had given him, throwing them to the floor behind the door which led from the hall into the dining room.

As he was doing this, one of the Justice agents seized him and placed him under arrest.

Within twenty minutes following Rabell's arrest, to our amazement, there dashed across my lawn, white of face and breathless, Mr. John J. Burns, General Counsel of the Securities and Exchange Commission at Washington! Mr. Burns' headquarters were in Washington—his home in Boston, Massachusetts. How did he ever happen to be so nearby while Rabell was conducting his operations in my home? Why did he arrive with a look of consternation on his face and in obviously agitated frame of mind?

Mr. Fischbach stepped outside to greet the Commission's Counsellor as he approached the door. Burns' first words, spoken almost in gasping man-

ner—as he ignored even the giving of response to
my counsel's greetings, were: "Just how far am I
involved in this thing, Fischbach?"

But the General Counsel soon left my premises,
as the Department of Justice Agents took Rabell
to New York City. Rabell there was imprisoned
until bail had been arranged for him, following his
indictment by a Federal Grand Jury on charges of
soliciting and accepting a bribe to influence his testimony as a government witness.

Having in mind that it was I who had instructed
my own men to record the Rabell conversations,
that it was I who had communicated with the authorities prior to those conversations, that it was
I who had talked with Assistant United States Attorney Murphy of the Department of Justice on the
night of Friday, June 21st, following the first recorded conversation, and that it was I who had arranged with Mr. Murphy for the two Department
of Justice Agents to be present at my home on Sunday for the second recording, and that I had never
discussed any of these arrangements with Burns or
with anybody else of the Commission, and that
Burns was not present at my home at all until about
twenty minutes after Rabell had been arrested, I
was greatly amazed to read a "Release in the Morning Newspapers of Tuesday, June 25, 1935," issued

by the Securities and Exchange Commission and entitled "Release No. X."

The "Release" concerned the Rabell affair. It, of course, was published in the press for the benefit, presumably, of the American public. It stated that the Commission, only a few days before, had requested the resignation of "Mr. Rabell, whose application indicated broad experience!"

I accepted that "resignation" story fairly willingly as about the only thing I could expect to hear. But I regarded some of the statements contained in the "Release," as strange and unusual distortion of the facts. I released no publicity statement, however, to the effect that such "appeared" to me as "untrue statements of material facts or omissions of material facts necessary in order to make the statements made, in the light of the circumstances under which they were made, not misleading." After all, I was dealing with the "Truth in Securities" Commission. I quote, however, the statements in question, with my own comment parenthetically stated as insertions within the Commission's statement.

"On June 22, the Commission, through confidential sources, received word that Mr. Rabell had approached one J. Edward Jones" (*the "approach" had been made several days before the first recorded conversation on June 21st).*

"The Commission immediately conferred with officials of the Federal Bureau of Investigation (*Department of Justice*) and requested their active coöperation. (*But the assistance of the Federal Bureau of Investigation already had been obtained by me from Assistant United States Attorney Murphy.*) At the interview which Mr. Jones had arranged with Mr. Rabell (*Rabell, not I, solicited the interviews*) at the former's home in Scarsdale, New York, on Friday, June 21st, and on Sunday, June 23rd, complete records of the conversations were recorded for use by the Department of Justice authorities. (*"Complete" records were made, it is true, but they were not made by Department of Justice authorities nor were they made expressly, as the "Release" implied, for their use. On the other hand, they were made at my personal direction, by my own paid staff of employees, for my own use and for my own protection on advice of counsel, and against what I feared was a "frame-up" against me by Rabell, Burns and Flynn.*) The Department of Justice Agents from the Southern District of New York and Judge John J. Burns, General Counsel of the Securities and Exchange Commission, were present at the meeting on the 23rd. (*This implies, of course, that the youthful "Judge" was on hand, bright and early, and that he personally took part in the proceedings, attending the recording of the conversation and that he, of course, being "present at the meeting" also took part in the capture of his own Assistant Chief and the arrest which followed. The statement made by the Commission that Burns was "present at the meeting" appears to be somewhat "misleading" since, indeed, he played quite a different role. He had arrived, out of breath, twenty minutes after the arrest of his confrere had been made, apparently fearing that he himself had been involved.)* Immediately after Sunday's meeting *(at which time the "Release" states Burns was present)* Rabell was taken into custody." *(But by authorities who were present, not by Burns who was absent!)*

These few paragraphs concerning the Commission's "Release No. X," while they may be passed over as inconsequential observations, nevertheless pertain to the Commission's "most effective weapon"—that of publicity, informing the great American public of the "Truth in Securities." Here is the "truth" torn naked. Here is a case where the public may have been given "news" which strangely implied "facts" that I felt never existed. For one might think, on reading the Commission's words above quoted, that young Burns was a prime factor in the capturing of his own lieutenant! Yet, I somehow felt that I had accomplished that feat and I now feel that honesty toward the public, fairness toward me and gentlemanly honor toward their own consciences, should have demanded from the Commission authorities, not cheap attempt at credit-taking, but dignified official quietude in such an unfortunate circumstance.

Rabell shortly was to be tried in court proceedings that resulted in a "hung" jury. He then was tried again, but the "Truth in Securities" Commission's representative, John Flynn, as the sole witness for the defense at the trial, testified under oath that the Commission did not, after all, intend to use this man, who, under Flynn's own urgings, had sworn to their affidavit against me, as a witness in my case! The Judge thereupon did not allow the case to go to the Jury for decision, but, instead, dismissed the indictment against Rabell because of the stated fact that the indictment charged him with having solicited and accepted money to influence his testimony as a government witness. Flynn's sworn testimony to the effect that the Commission was determined not to use Rabell as a witness, therefore saved the day for his erstwhile associate and Rabell again went free.

While I realized fully the noble purpose Congress had in mind in passing the laws that created the Securities and Exchange Commission, my unfortunate experience demonstrated the grave danger to personal liberties in this country in the creation of political agencies of government—a New Deal policeman, in the present instance, if I may—which can be used by officials to besmear and to ruin a man who had incurred the displeasure or antagonism of a high governmental official.

The ideals which gave birth to the Securities and Exchange Commission may be poorly served, if in the administration of the laws, ambitious young men, hitherto unknown, but eager to gain a reputation or newspaper publicity, become, alas, imbued with a vindictive spirit of personal animosity to ruin citizens and their businesses. The acts of the individuals so charged with the thrill of the "chase" are quite apt to become the invalid acts of irresponsible and unwise public officials. Such, of course, are not acts which were intended by the lawmakers.

Responsible officialdom, however, no matter how highly placed, should be firm in the imposition of restraints upon its subordinates, lest the civil liberties without which this government could not, in fact, long exist, be destroyed. The Supreme Court rightly sensed this great issue in my own case and, in its celebrated decision, struck hard at such dan-

ger in warning against the making of our nation a
government of men instead of one of laws. The
Court stated in my own decision that the "Constitutional safeguards of personal liberty ultimately
rest" upon the premise "that this shall be a government of laws;" and the Court warned that "to the
precise extent that the mere will of an official or
an official body is permitted to take the place of
allowable official discretion or to supplant the standing law as a rule of human conduct, the government
ceases to be one of laws and becomes an autocracy."

The expressions of the Court in my case upon
the right of the individual to protection from government bureaucracy were couched in most vigorous terms. The decision continued in these words:
"Our institutions must be kept free from the ap-
propriation of unauthorized power by lesser agencies," and, "if the various administrative bureaus
and commissions necessarily called and being called
into existence by the increasing complexities of our
modern business and political affairs, are permitted
gradually to extend their powers by encroachments,
even petty encroachments, upon the fundamental
rights, privileges and immunities of the people, we
shall, in the end, while avoiding the fatal consequences of a supreme autocracy, become submerged
by a multitude of minor invasions of personal

rights, less destructive but no less violative of constitutional guarantees."

But more of the type of thing to which I had been subjected was yet to come, and to an ever increasingly vicious degree.

CHAPTER XV

The Supreme Court Speaks!

On June 27th the adjourned hearing of the Commission's "stop-order" proceedings against me in connection with the Registration statement which Mr. Lundy had filed, opened in Washington to the usual accompaniment of complete arrangements for the accommodation of the press. Although I had been served with a subpoena requiring my attendance at this staged "affair," I did not regard the proceeding as a valid one and consequently refused to honor the subpoena by my personal appearance.

Inasmuch as I contended that I already, at the June 18th hearing, had effectively withdrawn my registration statement, I refused to attend the hearing but, instead, dispatched my Counsel, Mr. Fischbach and an oil lawyer, from Enid, Oklahoma, to appear for me.

My counsel submitted formal motions to dismiss the registration statement as well as the proceeding

itself, and to quash the subpoena which had been
served upon me at my offices in New York. These
motions, in quick and decisive manner, successively
were denied by the trial examiner of the Commission. Appropriate exceptions to these rulings were
noted on the record by my counsel who thereupon
again withdrew from the proceeding.

Lately American citizens have read in the public
press of what they have regarded as strange proceedings in Russian Soviet Courts. A glance at the
records made by some of the New Deal Commissions
in their functioning as quasi-judicial bodies will
bring America to the fore in the list of countries
possessing bureaucratic organs to exhibit strange
performances in dealings with individual liberty.

Aside from the general ruthlessness of the Securities and Exchange Commission in its tyrannical
abuses of power exhibited toward me, I often was
amused at the conduct of some of the young counsel
who represented the Commission, and as well, the
attitude of the "Judge" or trial examiner as he
demonstrated his judicial temperament and dignity
in the dispensation of his particular brand of "justice." In appraising the nature of the hearings, or
"trials" that are accorded those whom the Commission summons before it, and the press, as well,
it is advisable to remember that the trial examiner

is, in fact, simply a member of the legal staff of the Commission itself. He is subject, of course, to the orders of the Commission, on the payroll as such, but charged with the duty of rendering decisions regarding controversies between citizens and the Commission. The trial examiner sitting as "Judge" for my hearing, strange to say, was the same trial examiner who had sat in my first long hearings at New York and who, also, had spent considerable time in drawing the complaint against me, based upon Rabell's affidavit. In the Washington hearing, above described, an incident occurred which recorded a ludicrous "judicial" practice. At a certain point in the proceeding, the counsel for the Commission, a young Mr. Cohn, suddenly sprang to the bench and actually began to whisper into the "judge's" ear! The record thereupon shows the following:

Mr. Fischbach: I would like to know, Mr. Examiner, whether Mr. Cohn is now addressing you on any matter concerning this proceeding, and, if he is, I believe it should be on the record.

No comment is needed to emphasize an obvious point indicative of the danger that could flow from such "judicial" business. The conclusions which may be drawn from such type of procedure are left to the reader.

On the very next day, June 28th, 1935, I proceeded against the Securities and Exchange Commission by filing a petition in the United States Circuit Court of Appeals at New York, in which I asked the Court to review the action of the Commission in denying the motions I had filed before it.

A few days later, the Securities and Exchange Commission brought action against me in the United States District Court at New York to compel me to obey their subpoena to attend their hearing. I, of course, defended myself in this action, but lost on a decision by Judge Caffey who ordered me to obey the subpoena, remarking, in his decision, that, as I had not attended the hearing, I should not "kick" before I was "spurred."

As I did not wish, however, to be "spurred" any more, I made further "kick" in the form of an appeal from Judge Caffey's decision and his order was stayed pending the appeal.

Arguments duly were made in the United States Circuit Court of Appeals on a consolidation of the appeal from Judge Caffey's decision and the action which I had brought against the Commission, as well. I lost both actions in a decision which again upheld the Commission.

I thereupon instructed my Counsel to take the case to the United States Supreme Court for review of the decision of the lower Court, and during the next several months work in preparing the case went forward. My legal staff in this action comprised the late Honorable James M. Beck, noted Constitutional lawyer and former Solicitor General of the United States; the Honorable Bainbridge Colby, distinguished American statesman and Secretary of State in the Cabinet of President Woodrow Wilson; Mr. J. N. Saye, eminent oil lawyer of Longview, Texas, and Mr. Fischbach.

In the meantime, due to the tremendous amount of adverse publicity released by the Securities and Exchange Commission concerning me, my business became almost wholly stagnated to a point of ruination and my business organization was practically destroyed. I abandoned all my offices except that one in New York and became almost submerged with distress caused by financial worries and the great embarrassment that attended my struggle. My Executive Assistant, Mr. John G. Scattergood, a sensitive man of a very high sense of honor, within a few months succumbed to the public shame he felt from the Commission's attacks, to a point where, weakened by worry, he contracted a streptococcus infection and died in September, 1935, leaving a wife and three small boys to survive him. Mrs. Scattergood, his lawyer and his doctor all attributed his untimely death to the acts of the Commission.

Arguments duly were presented before the Supreme Court in Washington, and finally, on April 6th, 1936, the great decision of the Court was handed down. In this decision, the Court, speaking through Justice Sutherland, in strong and vigorous language, upheld the rights and liberties of individual citizens in this country as against the tyrannical abuses of power on the part of officials of the government. By a vote of 6 to 3, the Court reversed the lower Courts in their decisions against me and held that the Securities and Exchange Commission bureaucratically invaded my Constitutional rights. The Court denounced, in forceful language, bureaucracy by governmental agencies, adding that liberty in this country would be "submerged" in petty tyrannies if efforts such as those which represented the acts of the Securities and Exchange Commission went unchecked.

The majority ruling held that arbitrary power and the rule of the Constitution were antagonistic and incompatible forces, and that one or the other must perish.

The Court further declared that "the action of

the Commission finds no support in right principle or in law" and that "it is wholly unreasonable and arbitrary."

In condemning the Commission severely for violating "the cardinal precept upon which the Constitutional safeguards of personal liberty ultimately rest," the Court said that in the supplanting of the standing law by the mere will of an official, "the government ceases to be one of laws and becomes an autocracy."

"Arbitrary power and the rule of the Constitution cannot both exist," said the Court which, in quoting a decision concerning a "fishing expedition," further declared that: "An investigation not based upon specific grounds is quite as objectionable as a search warrant not based upon specified statements of fact.

"Such an investigation, or such a search, is unlawful in its inception," the Court held, and, condemning specifically the action of the Commission, stated: "If the action here of the Commission be upheld, it follows that production and inspection may be forced not only of books and private papers of the guilty, but those of the innocent as well, notwithstanding the proceedings for registration, so far as the Commission is concerned, has been brought to an end by the complete and legal withdrawal of the registration statement."

The decision of the Supreme Court was handed down on that April 6th, 1936, before a crowded court room that held a group of astonished Securities and Exchange Commission lawyers who were present as very much surprised and disappointed visitors. Great publicity throughout the land followed the decision.

But the New Deal was not slow. On the very next morning, April 7th, 1936, at ten o'clock, the United States Attorney went before a Federal Grand Jury in the City of New York to indict me!

CHAPTER XVI

New Deal at Work

The Securities and Exchange Commission delivered to the United States Attorney at New York, books, records and private papers which that Commission had obtained in the raid they conducted on my offices through the medium of their man Rabell, operating under the direction of Flynn. The Commission also delivered to the United States Attorney the affidavit of Rabell and the complaint and papers constituting the case which they had built against me in the old injunction proceeding that followed the operations of the Commission described in the quoted words of Rabell in a previous chapter.

The United States Attorney, Mr. Lamar Hardy, newly appointed by President Roosevelt, presented the case, through an assistant, to the Grand Jurors who, in turn, handed up their indictment on May 8, 1936, charging me with violation of the mail fraud statute, a penitentiary offense, if proved.

Great publicity resulted from this charge and press headlines and stories carried the startling news of an indictment that contained fifteen separate counts against me! My children, Edward, twelve, and Cathryn, fifteen, read in the papers that five years for each count, or a total of seventy-five years in the penitentiary, might be their father's penalty. On reading the indictment, however, I learned that each count was similar to every other, the basis for the fifteen counts being simply fifteen different routine letters which had been mailed by my organization. It so happened that not one of these letters had been written by me personally, but by subordinates of our office in the ordinary routine of their work. But I was the only defendant, however, no conspiracy of several individuals, as often is the case in such actions, being charged. It appeared as if J. Edward Jones was the only one hunted!

God forbid that any reader of these lines, through any possible quirk of fate, should be indicted by his government! The laws of this country, lawyers and the courts themselves say, are such that one accused is presumed to be innocent until proven guilty. I have found the practical effect of an accusation to be exactly the reverse; one, indicted, really is presumed by his fellow man to be guilty until proved to be innocent. And, even then, after complete vindication has been fully established and innocence proven in a public trial on the merits of the case, the scars that remain from the deep and damaging cuts received in such encounter, are there forever to stay as permanent labels—to damage one's standing; to hurt sensitive feelings of pride; to dampen hope and aspirations; to question the sincerity of friendly encouragement even from one's best friends; to create doubt of all humanity; to build bitterness in the heart against nearly everything "government;" to enhance continued worry; to develop a frantic state of mind that can visualize nothing constructive but, instead, only destruction of all ideals previously held high as the great goals of a life. I can say that the persecution attendant such terrible attack as an indictment by one's own government, is ruinous. This is said, now, in the matured belief that the individuals of the government who promoted my indictment never have realized the full extent of the consequences of their acts.

A man can, from depths of his despair, take his mind from the ruination of a business built upon a lifetime of work; and, likewise, from the destruction of his business organization which for years has been his pride; he can face threatened financial ruin

—even what seems to be the destruction of all hope for the rehabilitation of his business; but he cannot forget his worries and the sleepless nights of floor-walking that haunt his every thought, every hope of himself and those for whom life has made him responsible. Even as I write these words, sickness, resulting from continued aggravations caused by many months of worry, has weakened and destroyed health in my immediate family.

Immediately following the rush that brought my indictment so soon after the Supreme Court had spoken in my favor, the United States District Attorney adopted the policy of delaying a trial of the charges that had been made against me. Steadily and in routine manner, on or about the first of each succeeding month, the government regularly appeared in Court, asked and was given an adjournment of the case until the following month.

In the meantime, clients of mine were visited, questioned, summoned before the United States Attorney and, of course, in many cases made exceedingly apprehensive concerning their relations with me. My representatives in the oil fields likewise were examined and put to such fright concerning their relationship with me that shortly I was absolutely without any direct field representation whatsoever.

At the time, I had undertaken the development of some considerable oil property in the State of Louisiana, necessitating the drilling of several deep oil wells. I contracted the drilling of the wells with several drilling contractors, only to learn, to my great dismay, that such individuals subsequently were haled before representatives of the government and subjected to a searching line of inquisition—all to result in the cancellation of the drilling contracts that I had negotiated. This condition of affairs developed to a point where I found myself almost estopped in my efforts to do any operating in the fields at all—so concerned did my field operators become at what seemed to be an almost endless continuation of "investigation" of my affairs and activities. It will be understood, too, that such inquiries had no relation whatsoever to the charges made in the indictment rendered against me.

In addition to these official acts of my government, I was made the target of many persons—some of whom were highly placed in personal relationships either with political channels or with persons prominently identified with powerful individuals in the government. At all times, offers were made by these individuals to have the attacks which had been made against me called off and the indictment quashed; providing, of course, I paid such sources substantial sums of money. My experiences in connection with these persons brought home to me the important part graft plays in the very highest planes of activity surrounding our government.

The sorry chapters recorded by Rabell, of the Securities and Exchange Commission, for instance, were completely eclipsed, just a little later, by two different gentlemen—among others one, a "Colonel" Myles A. Lasker, who introduced himself—exhibiting as he did so, original signed contracts to prove it—as the Radio Business Manager for Eleanor Roosevelt, wife of the President; and the other, a John J. O'Donnell, representative of nothing less than the Democratic National Committee! The qualifications which these two men of high position advanced to convince me of their ability to perform the services they wished to sell, the stories related by them designed to prove to me the power and influence they wielded—all were so startling in the profundity of their significance that they left me with a revolting realization of a condition of affairs that seemed to me to need, and to need badly, a thoroughgoing and purefying investigation of itself!

CHAPTER XVII

New Dealirium

During the summer of 1936, I was approached by many different individuals who had some very strange proposals to make to me. On advice of counsel, and having in mind also the value of the recordings of the Rabell conversations, I caused to be installed in my office recording apparatus that could be used to make phonographic records of conversations had there.

I made these preparations as a precautionary measure in my own protection against what caution suggested might be a wise measure to forestall any possible attempt to misconstrue the meanings of or to misquote my own words.

Accordingly, on the occasion of visits by persons whom I regarded as possible governmental representatives, as extortionists, or "fixers," I made use of the recording equipment. Without laborious elaboration concerning many recordings made, the purpose of this book can be served by referring only to "Colonel" Myles Lasker, and Mr. John J.

O'Donnell. If perchance, any serious question be raised as to the authenticity of the record as quoted by me, arrangements may be made for the hearing, on loud speaker, of the actual voices in conversation. I have found that the phonographic needle, unlike, sometimes, the human tongue, does not wabble when actual fact is wanted, but that it relates its story truthfully from the record. In this instance, I have the records.

One day, a young man I had not known before, visited me at my office and offered to introduce me to a person who, it was stated, represented himself as having a definite contractual relationship with the wife of the President of the United States and also with having influence with the powerful Presidential Secretariat. I was urged to go to see the gentleman in question, one Myles Lasker, who, I was advised, wished to make my acquaintance and who no doubt could "do something" for me. I, of course, intrigued by the suggestion, was desirous of learning how far this kind of business might go. I, therefore, went with my new found friend to Mr. Lasker's office, about a block from that of my own.

On meeting Mr. Lasker, self-styled "Colonel" with big eyes, heavy, well-filled frame, and deep husky voice, I perceived a tendency on his part toward loquacity characterized by a free and familiar reference to personnel known to be identified closely with the White House, obviously, as I thought, to impress me with his high connections.

He very promptly produced for my inspection certain contracts which were sealed by the original signatures of Eleanor Roosevelt and himself. He advised me that he was the "Radio Manager" for the First Lady and that he was in position to speak with her at any time and on any subject.

He took occasion to exhibit to me some check vouchers showing that many thousands of dollars had been paid to him by one of the large oil companies, which money, he pointed out to me, had been given to him for special services he had been able to render through his Washington connections in thwarting the purposes of Governmental agencies in the making of investigations and the handling of reports concerning the activities of the corporation in question.

With such apparent attempt to qualify for his ability to perform, our conversation naturally reverted to my own troubles and the "Colonel," in sympathetic style, held himself open to help me as best he could, stating that it would be necessary, because of his very high connections, to "keep it on the up and up."

An appointment was made for the Colonel to come to my own office, where, it was agreed, we could have ample opportunity to go fully into the matter.

The Colonel arrived at my office at about seven o'clock on the stormy evening of August 13th.

At the outset of our conversation I asked what his services in my behalf would cost me and he said that about $2,000 would be required for "expenses," and $25,000 was finally stated as "a fair fee."

"I would say, offhand, if you put it up to me," said Colonel Lasker, "that a fee of $25,000.00 would be a fair fee."

The Colonel seemed particularly desirous that I regard his proposition to me as one made on a very high level. He took special pains to warn me against any thought that he would be concerned with graft.

"It's got to be above board," said the Colonel, "or I don't want any part of it. I'm getting cured of playing with fire! I don't believe in what is called graft, not at all!"

But, apparently sensing a way out, if any question might arise as to the ethics of what he had to propose, the esteemed Colonel, in a striking pose of innocence, said, " . . . I'll even do this, if undue influences were brought to bear I would allow you to hire me as your Public Relations Counsel for one year at a salary of $25,000.00 a year and whatever other publicity expenses there are."

In stating further how he wished me to regard him as well as how *not* to regard him, Col. Lasker said:

"I do want you to get one thought in your mind or out of your mind—either way. I don't want you to ever think of me as a 'fixer,' because that's the one thing that I'm not."

Mr. Jones: Well, I don't know anything about the way you function, I don't know you.

Col. Lasker: I mean, I just don't—I don't want to be known as that. As big a job of public relations as any other is the fact of being able to square things—to square things.

In speaking of the indictment, Colonel Lasker assured me that, through his influences, he could have it dismissed.

"It is going to be dismissed," declared the Colonel, "there is no question about it. I do feel, I may be all wrong, but I do feel that I can have it dismissed, but it's going to mean a lot of work."

And then as if by way of qualifying himself further, Mr. Lasker related a story of amazing import! He told me that for a very substantial fee, he had been retained by a big public utility man of Chicago, who had employed him to put a stop to an investigation which the United States Senate had launched into the utility man's affairs. And in the relation of his story he indicated that he had thwarted the purpose of the United States Senate by using his influence with the Presidential Secretariat and that, through his ability "to put in a word with Black" (then United States Senator Black, who headed the Senatorial Investigating Committee—now Associate Justice Black of the United States Supreme Court) the investigation had "fizzled off to nothing." In this connection the following colloquy is pertinent:

Col. Lasker: I got Harley Clarke out of his investigation down there.

Mr. Jones: Who's that?

Col. Lasker: Harley Clarke.

Mr. Jones: Clarke Brothers Bank—that closed?

Col. Lasker: No. Harley Clarke is the man who heads big utilities, and Harley Clarke wrote me a very substantial check.

Mr. Jones: What did you do for him?

Col. Lasker: Well, I connected with his investigation down there before a Senatorial Committee. I was able to put in a word with Black, so that the whole thing just fizzled off to nothing.

Mr. Jones: Did you do that through the same channels that—

Col. Lasker: I did it when Louie Howe was alive down there, and Harley Clarke, as I say, paid me a very nice check, a fee which, unfortunately, I had to share with some other people.

The Colonel seemed to think that his performance in the Clarke case had resulted in the successful handling of a problem much more intricate or difficult than that which mine would represent.

Mr. Jones: How long do you think it will take to get it knocked out?

Col. Lasker: With luck, in a week.

Mr. Jones: Have you ever had anything as bad as that knocked out? An indictment?

Col. Lasker: Well, I think this Harley Clarke case was even worse.

Mr. Jones: I'm not familiar with that case. Were they after him?

Col. Lasker: Every which way!

Mr. Jones: They were? Of course, my name is "mud" with some of the people down there in Washington.

Col. Lasker: That's all right. We'll take care of that.

The Colonel urged me to go, personally, with him to the White House, at Washington, when, he stated, he would take up the matter with his friend Steve Early, who had great influence with the President.

Col. Lasker: Steve Early has charge of all the press relations for the President, so on and so forth. Secretary, as you know, to the President. He has a tremendous amount of influence with the President. Tremendous. Since Louie Howe died, I should say that Steve has sort of walked into Louie's shoes.

The Colonel then told me he would urge Mr. Early to take my matter to the President, or to Mr. Cummings, in order to get my case "dropped." Then he predicted having the case knocked out "in a week."

Another sidelight on how an individual, so intimately placed as was Colonel Lasker, viewed the possibility of easy "fixing" is shown by comment made by the Colonel about one Ralph Steinberg, described as a "powerful man," connected with the Democratic Committee.

Col. Lasker: And I'll go to a man who is very powerful. He happens to be up here at the Biltmore. Steinberg.

Mr. Jones: Who's that?

Col. Lasker: Ralph Steinberg.

Mr. Jones: I don't know him. Is he working for the Committee?

Col. Lasker: That's right. And that would probably mean that I would have to give Ralph part of my fee, but Ralph can do lots of things that I can't do, but as far as fixing is concerned, that all means money.

Mr. Jones: Is he connected with Cummings?

Col. Lasker: He is connected with the Democratic Committee, and has nothing to do with Cummings, but he can walk into any one of the Cabinet offices as I can walk into the White House.

Mr. Jones: Yeah? Well, then your plan is first to go to Early?

Col. Lasker: Yes.

The Colonel then referred to an investigation launched by the Black Senatorial Investigating Committee of Cities Service Company, referring, also, to payments made by that company to him for his "services"—the vouchers for which he actually had showed to me in his own office.

Mr. Jones: How did you ever keep the S.E.C. off the Henry L. Doherty business?

Col. Lasker: Well, it was real hard work.

Mr. Jones: The S.E.C.—I thought they landed on everybody!

Col. Lasker: No. It was real hard work that was done and up to the time the Black Committee started investigating Cities Service I was on that payroll for a retainer each month. A very lovely retainer at that—they used me when they wanted me. If they wanted me, they used me. Three times in the first year that I was with them. Twice the second year—twice the third year and once the fourth.

Mr. Jones: From the check vouchers you had there —my God, you must have spent a lot of money for them some place.

Col. Lasker: That was money that they gave me for my services.

Mr. Jones: Yes?

Col. Lasker: Now, they paid me as I said, one year, $30,000, then $25,000, to $30,000 for the fourth year.

The Colonel assured me that he knew what he could do and that he had been and still was quite intimate with the affairs of White House personages.

Col. Lasker: What I tell you is definitely what I can put across.

Mr. Jones: Well, now, of course, you are in close, on the inside of the Roosevelt family, as I understand it. And what are you for Eleanor Roosevelt?

Col. Lasker: I handle all of her radio broadcasts, as Public Relations Counsel.

Mr. Jones: Publicity to newspapers?

Col. Lasker: No, I don't handle any of that.

Mr. Jones: How do you get your influence with Early?

Col. Lasker: Well, I handled all of Louie Howe's private business, when Louie Howe was alive. Steve and I have been friends for a good many years.

Mr. Jones: Well, you'd recommend that I go down there and have a talk with him?

Col. Lasker: I would, in your case.

Mr. Jones: Do you think that he will bring it to the attention of Cummings?

Col. Lasker: I do. I certainly do.

At another point in our conversation I pressed the Colonel as to whether he knew that Mr. Early really possessed sufficient influence to do the thing Col. Lasker represented he could have done and I received the most positive assurances that the White House Secretary definitely could accomplish that purpose.

Mr. Jones: Do you think that Early will have enough influence?

Col. Lasker: Oh, definitely.

Mr. Jones: . . . to bring about the dismissal of—
Col. Lasker: Definitely.
Mr. Jones: You're sure?
Col. Lasker: Oh, positively. I have nothing to worry about.

At the outset of my conversation with Lasker, I really had a desire to lay before either the President or Mr. Cummings, what I regarded as the iniquities of a deliberate persecution of me—still thinking that possibly I could prevail upon someone high in authority to call a halt to what I then felt eventually would result in defeat for the government, even though I were to be ruined. In face of such a desire, I, nevertheless, was suspicious of the legitimacy of the proposals which I might receive from Lasker.

While the recorded conversation was proceeding, I decided to follow, just a little further, the suggestions which had been made to me and to learn, if possible, how bold this particular new scheme might become. Accordingly, I agreed to fly with Col. Lasker to Washington on the coming day.

I arranged for my counsel, Mr. Fischbach, to accompany us and, on arriving at the Capital, the Colonel promptly telephoned the White House, whereupon an appointment with Mr. Early readily was made for him. I decided not to go to the

White House, but sent Mr. Fischbach in my stead, instructing him to observe the treatment accorded Colonel Lasker and to formulate, in his own mind, and from his own observations, plans I should follow and to be prepared to advise me later whether any possible legitimate chance might exist to warrant a continuation of my association with the Colonel.

Secretary Early, of the White House, sent Col. Lasker and Mr. Fischbach to the office of the Attorney General of the United States, where, Mr. Fischbach reported, the two were advised that the matter would be taken up with the United States Attorney in New York by a personal visit on the part of an assistant to the Attorney General himself.

The advice, however, which my counsel later, on our return home, gave me was for me to discontinue forthwith all further contacts with the esteemed Colonel, since, Mr. Fischbach advised, no legitimate purpose, in his opinion, could be accomplished through such channel.

I, of course, promptly ended all further association with Lasker. But wonder has never since left my mind concerning the possible danger to good government of this country, if conditions such as Lasker described could exist.

He had specifically stated that he worked through

the White House. In emphasizing his power, he had pointed a finger at the possibility that a genuine purpose of the United States Senate, in investigating what seemed to be important matters, had been thwarted through his powerful contacts. He strongly implied that money had been used in surreptitious manner to bring about such contingency. He was closely identified, even through contracts, with very prominent personages and his statements, therefore, naturally demanded some respect.

Purely as a matter of public concern, it would, I believe, be interesting, and, no doubt, helpful, as well, if the full facts of all that Lasker related to me, could only be made known. If any Senator, no matter how highly placed at this time, ever gave improper heed to a "few words" from the handsomely paid Lasker, the Senate, itself, should be informed of all the influences—no matter from what source exerted—that can work in Washington to nullify genuine purpose of that body in investigating matters its good conscience suggests should be investigated. A denial of such purpose strikes deep at the very roots of the only kind of government that long can endure among a free people.

But an even more dangerous and disgraceful element shortly was to make itself known to me in presenting a shocking proposal that caused me quickly to refer the matter to the Federal Authorities for proper handling. Big national politics stooped low for money wanted! Further revelations were to be forthcoming that pictured national figures indulging in practices unworthy even of the cheapest of ward politics!

CHAPTER XVIII

Books for Sale!

During the two months following the Lasker proposals, the Presidential Campaign of 1936 warmed to a very considerable degree. The general headquarters of the Democratic National Committee, ensconced in the Biltmore Hotel across the street from my New York offices, swarmed with loyal party workers who shouted their praises for the political purposes of the great New Dealer—a candidate to succeed himself.

As time rolled along, I was steadily shadowed, my telephone wires were tapped at intermittent intervals and, as the months went by, my trial on the indictment which had been rendered so hurriedly against me, constantly was subjected to adjournment, the United States Attorney requesting additional postponement each month.

In the oil fields, "investigations" of my current efforts continued. In this particular respect, however, I had been enabled, through the friendly act of a good citizen, to start a substantial drilling pro-

gram. Such a stroke of good fortune came from a
Samaritan from Texas. On being informed by me
of my difficulties in obtaining drillers because of the
insistence by governmental representatives upon
scrutinizing drilling contracts and "investigating"
the drillers' connections with me, this gentleman
promptly agreed to drill 6,000 foot oil wells for me
on my own word and without a "scratch of paper"
between us. The coöperation in this kind of a new
deal on the part of this very splendid individual
soon permitted me to discover a new and big oil
pool, and I shall always be gratefully indebted to
Mr. Tom Potter, of Kilgore, Texas, for the honor of
a lasting friendship with a real man.

Confronted as I was with my difficulties, caused
by those persons of the government who so stooped
to snoop, I became immediately wary on receiving
on one Tuesday, October 20th, a telephone call announced as coming direct from the headquarters of
the great Democratic National Committee! The
caller introduced himself as one John J. O'Donnell,
stated that he was speaking from the Democratic
National Headquarters, "just across the street," and
asked for an appointment to see me.

Taken aback, somewhat, by this new gesture from
such a mighty source, I expressed my surprise that,
in view of my own difficulties with the administra-

tion, anyone connected with the Democratic National Committee should wish to see me. I was assured by O'Donnell, however, that before he would be through with me I would be "wearing a Roosevelt button."

Even buttons were beginning to be somewhat scarce with me, so I told my Democrat that he could come over to my office. In no time at all he was there: rotund, tenor voice, smiles all over a professionally friendly face.

O'Donnell promptly began to reveal to me how the Democratic Committee had devised a scheme to permit them to evade compliance with the Federal law respecting contributions to political campaigns. Along with such information, he advanced an astounding proposal whereby I might, through the Committee, buy myself out of the troubles the government had heaped upon me! This could be done, he said, providing I would "coöperate" with the Democratic National Committee by giving them money for some old, out of date convention books. The transaction, in O'Donnell's own words, being, not a campaign "contribution," but a "blind," instead!

During the whole of my life, I always had the greatest respect for the majesty of the law and of my own Government. Since the days, first remembered by me, when early in infancy, I rumbled across the Kansas state line in a prairie schooner, my parents patriotically had taught a conception of America that eschewed any thought other than that the highest of motives always guided the purpose and functioning of the great American Government. The ideal of that government, in fact, was conceived by my parents to be one always characterized by the highest plane of honor; a government, if you please, to respect; to honor; to defend, if need should arise, with one's last effort.

Even now, I like to forget an experience that revealed to me sordid realities of a long and bitter struggle, and, instead, still bask in the idealistic conceptions taught of a great government. Such conceptions, I believe, absorbed the minds of the founding fathers when they established the American system of government, because there seems to be little provision in our charter of government to protect against the possibility that, perchance, through the falling into the hands of cheap politicians, the government, itself, might be turned to purposes other than honorable. If, indeed, any great weakness exists in the system originally established as our very own, it well may be found in the fact that, in principle, an ideal founded upon a basis of honor, but, through fate, allowed to be manipulated or administered by elements imbued with baser motives, may fall an easy tool to the destruction even of those fundamental principles which it was, in fact, designed to perpetuate.

As I admire and love the great principles and ideals upon which the American governmental system is based, I despise the invalid acts of unwise or vindictive governmental officials, and, as well, the lowly purposes of "fixers," grafters and cheap politicians whose acts and practices I believe to be subversive of the high motives and purposes of our Federal government. In that attitude, I believe, also, that good citizenship requires the exposing of anything at all which may prove to be inimical to the best interests of our government. As a matter of fact, in that very conviction, lies the reason for the writing of this book.

When the representative of the Democratic National Committee first came into my private office I at once demanded to be informed as to the purpose of his visit, asking these words. "What do you have on your mind?"

Inasmuch as I personally had been indicted for an alleged scheme in violation of law, I was surprised to be informed that the Democratic National Committee had a scheme to obtain money under the false pretense of selling merchandise instead of accepting campaign contributions, "as such." The plan, or artifice, I was advised, had been formulated as a means by which funds could be procured by the Democrats in a manner to defy revelation by investigation on the part of the United States Senate—a scheme by which the law that requires full reports of all contributions, could be evaded, or violated, by the clever subterfuge of creating a "blind" for such contributions in the form of a "sale" of books or merchandise, which no law requires to be reported.

In answer to my question O'Donnell immediately asked me to "coöperate" with the Democratic National Committee.

Mr. O'Donnell: Well, now, here's the way that we'd like to get you to coöperate with us.

Mr. Jones: Coöperate with you?

Mr. O'Donnell: We've got this Democratic National Convention Book. The only reason for its being in existence is to have the committee know that they're with them in spirit—purchase books! They can buy merchandise. It's not a contribution to the— (in confidential tone) it's a contribution to the campaign but it isn't the type open to Senatorial investigation.

My nerves being just a little frayed by "investigations" of many sorts, I ejaculated:

> "Gee, I don't want any Senatorial investigation!"

The National Committee's "book salesman" was thereupon quick to define the virtue of the Democratic scheme and to alleviate my fear.

Mr. O'Donnell: Not anything of that sort. A contribution, as such, to the campaign—they have to make a list; but, with the books, they just report "so many books sold."
Mr. Jones: Right smart of them.
Mr. O'Donnell: Because we're selling them all over the country and we have men that don't want any publicity and that is the method in which we—that's the only reason for this thing being in existence. . . .

As O'Donnell pointed out to me how a purchaser shielded from Senatorial exposé, avoided even the public eye given to those who placed advertisements in the book, I asked,

> "Why do you come to me when I've been so pursued and persecuted and hounded by the New Deal Administration that I just—"

I was interrupted by his

"Well, now, here's the point . . . "

Mr. Jones: You are connected with the Democratic National Committee.

Mr. O'Donnell: I'm in charge of the Democrats of the metropolitan area.

Mr. Jones: How many people have you got who don't want publicity—what kind of a deal is made?

Mr. O'Donnell: Plenty, if you ask me.

Mr. Jones: Plenty? Not in as bad a situation as I'm in, have you?

Mr. O'Donnell: Yes. . . . probably 1,000, so far.

Mr. Jones: Contributors who want a little—

Mr. O'Donnell: They buy merchandise. They say, "All right, we like the book." It's a very fine —the book contains a history of the last four years and we think it's a very nice thing.

Mr. Jones: A nice book.

Mr. O'Donnell: Yes, it's a nice book, and "we feel that you should distribute those among the worthy Democrats in spots where it'll do the most good. I'll underwrite so many copies of the book." They write their own check. They're making it in the form of a contribution, but actually they're buying merchandise. They get a receipt; I give you a receipt.

Mr. Jones: You say that there's no Senatorial Investigation—?

Mr. O'Donnell: Oh, no. But—the only thing is, those records are kept very confidential. They have to be because we have been—I mean, men have given to this and they said, "Now this is absolutely confidential." There's no one but Mr. Farley and Forbes Morgan that know anything about this.

Mr. Jones: And they instruct you to keep it confidential?

Mr. O'Donnell: Oh, yes—by all means . . . The orders go right into their office . . . and the checks; and it's acknowledged. . . . I'll give you a letter on Democratic stationery bearing Farley's and Morgan's signature.

Mr. Jones: Is that so?

Mr. O'Donnell: Your check goes to the Committee. You get a receipt from the Treasurer's office that you have purchased so many books for so much money.

Mr. Jones: Treasurer of what?

Mr. O'Donnell: Treasurer of the Democratic National Committee.

Mr. Jones: Well, to whom do I draw my check?

Mr. O'Donnell: To the Democratic National Committee.

Mr. Jones: And they keep it confidential?

Mr. O'Donnell: Absolutely.

Mr. Jones: Then—and you say to me that that is not subject to a Senatorial investigation?

Mr. O'Donnell: It is not because it isn't a contribution to the campaign as such. You will purchase books.

Mr. Jones: I see.

Mr. O'Donnell: You purchase merchandise, see?

Mr. Jones: Who thought that one up?

Mr. O'Donnell: Well, it's "one of those things. . . . "

Mr. Jones: Well, that's a means of getting money without having it made subject to—

Mr. O'Donnell (interrupting): Correct. Now, here's the point.

Mr. Jones: To a Congressional investigation.

Mr. O'Donnell: Correct. And it's a nice gesture on your part. It shows the Committee at least you're thinking of them in the campaign.

Mr. Jones: Don't you know what they've done to me, this administration?

Mr. O'Donnell: Yes . . . you're in a spot. I mean—it's not too bad, it's one of those—

Mr. Jones: Well, I'm certainly in a spot. You've got me right, there.

Mr. O'Donnell: Yes—well, I—

Mr. Jones: Will it do me any good?

And so, the scheme of the Democratic National Committee to get around the law in the obtaining of money, and to avoid publicity by the route of a Senatorial investigation had been outlined as an artifice that clearly put the Committee out of the business of soliciting campaign contributions and into the business of selling an out of date political "Convention" book that, long since, served its purpose at the rollicking, ballyhooing Philadelphia meeting of the Democrats months before.

O'Donnell unfolded to me, in an apparent attempt to be confidential, the real reason why he had come to see me. "Personally," he said, "I'll tell you why I'm in here. I'm a very good friend of Keith Morgan. Do you know Keith?"

Mr. Jones: No, I don't know him.

Mr. O'Donnell: He's one of the closest friends of the President in the South. He's got to be in this picture.

Mr. Jones: He's close to the President?

Mr. O'Donnell: Very close.

Mr. Jones: Now, do you work through him?

Mr. O'Donnell: Occasionally.

Mr. Jones: And would you work through him in my case?

Mr. O'Donnell: I certainly would. I'd take it through him. I think the more you have batting for you the better off you are.

Mr. Jones: Well, can you get all of this array of

good, powerful Democrats here to go to the
bat for me? How can you do that?

Mr. *O'Donnell*: I'll have it worked through Keith
Morgan.

Mr. *Jones*: Think he can do it?

Mr. *O'Donnell*: Yes, I know he can.

O'Donnell advised me that the book purchase
plan was the way to get things done. "Have it confirmed," he instructed, "and, the day after election,
step right into headquarters and say, 'Now, boys,
what are you gonna do for me?' "

Mr. *Jones*: You said they can do something.

Mr. *O'Donnell*: Yes, that's right.

Mr. *Jones*: Before I give you any money, I want to
know what you're going to do for me.

O'Donnell hinted strongly that if I made a purchase of the books he was offering I could have the
services of powerful individuals, either of the Democratic Committee or closely affiliated with it, in
having my troubles with the government ended.
He said he couldn't, at the time, promise me in
writing, but he did advise me what was necessary
for me to do in order to obtain the powerful influence he insisted would be available to me, providing, of course, I made the purchase.

Mr. O'Donnell: Here's what I think. Here's the thing that I want you to do and I think it would be a d—ned good thing for you to do.

Mr. Jones: All right, out with it.

Mr. O'Donnell: Underwrite a thousand of these books.

Mr. Jones: How much are they apiece?

Mr. O'Donnell: $2.50 a copy.

Mr. Jones: That's $2500.00. Two thousand five hundred dollars. Supposing I give you two thousand five hundred dollars. What will you do for me?

O'Donnell told me that on the very day after the election he would be at my services, stating it in these words:

"Now, I will—the day after election—I'll step right to the bat for you."

The "book salesman" was evasive as to exact promises, but he continued to assure me that if I would but advance the money he sought, I could depend on being taken care of immediately after the election. In face of my requests for a categorical statement from him, or a letter from somebody else of the Committee, he insisted that he could not actually go on record to the effect that "everything will be white-washed."

But I asked this cog of a smooth-running, well-oiled machine, "Why, that's what you're implying by this conversation."

Mr. O'Donnell: But that can't be done in that— in so many words.

Mr. Jones: You mean you can't put it on record that way?

Mr. O'Donnell: That's the idea.

Following the price quotations made by O'Donnell for the books the Democrats had for "sale," he phrased in his own way what I could expect by stating that the Committee would be "glad to run an errand" for me.

"Underwrite a thousand of those books," said Mr. O'Donnell, "of which you want one hundred here, or twenty, or fifty, or two hundred. The Committee can send the rest where it will do the most good, at their discretion."

"After that," he continued, "if you ask the Committee for a favor after election, we'll be glad to run an errand for you. Let me put it that way."

Mr. Jones: Now all right. If I give you two thousand five hundred, you'll be glad "to run an errand" for me.

Mr. O'Donnell: That's right.

Mr. Jones: Now, just between you and me, you'd

get somebody in the Committee, Morgan, or
whoever he is—

Mr. O'Donnell: That's right.

Mr. Jones: . . . to do the necessary things with
Lamar Hardy down here to get my case *nolle
prossed*—is that what you mean?

Mr. O'Donnell: I'll do my damnedest.

I was advised that the transaction would be kept
so confidential that the United States Senate could
not get at the records. And the famous Mr. Farley,
along with the Democratic Treasurer, would be
the guardians of the secret!

Mr. Jones: Well, who would know that I made a
contribution to this—

Mr. O'Donnell: Mr. Farley and Mr. Morgan.

Mr. Jones: That I did the buying?

Mr. O'Donnell: Because they would know it.
They'd know about it immediately.

Mr. Jones: Mr. Farley would know it?

Mr. O'Donnell: And Mr. Morgan.

And I asked this esteemed representative of the
nation's dominant political party that even then, in
campaign battling was condemning chicanery,
hypocrisy, graft and fraud, the following:

"And you say to me, that if I do that you think
my case will be forced out?"

And the representative of that which is good in Government again replied, "I'll do my damnedest!"

O'Donnell then exhibited a copy of the famous book, exclaiming as he produced it, "It's a beautiful thing—if you can conceive this thing."

And as I turned the pages I observed, on viewing the pictures of many of those Democrats who held the highest positions of honor capable of being bestowed by a trusting people: "I guess it's a good book. There's the President of the United States to start it off with."

Mr. Jones: Does he, does Roosevelt know anything about the way this book is merchandised?

Mr. O'Donnell: You bet your life he does, and he approved it!

Mr. Jones: He approved it?

Mr. O'Donnell: Yes, he's approved it. Why he was sore because the liquor ads went in these and then finally he let it go.

Mr. Jones: Does he know it's a sort of blind for contributions?

Mr. O'Donnell: Why, sure he does. Can't be anything else!

And, on observing other pictures—

Mr. Jones: There's Homer Cummings. Does he know about this book?

Mr. O'Donnell: I should say he does. He posed specially for that photograph.

Mr. Jones: For this photograph?

Mr. O'Donnell: Yes.

Mr. Jones: Posed specially for a photograph for this "blind for contributions"?

Mr. O'Donnell: (Laughing) Certainly!

Mr. Jones: He shouldn't do a thing like that.
(More laughter by O'Donnell.)
That's terrible.

Mr. Jones: (reading aloud)
"Department of Justice by Homer Cummings, Attorney General." Posed especially for this "blind alley" book. Can you beat that?

And as we ran through the pages to beam upon many familiar faces of those only recently made great—

Mr. Jones: Here's Mr. Farley. Did he pose specially for that?

Mr. O'Donnell: I guess he did.

And after looking over the entire panorama of greatness—

Mr. O'Donnell: Now, there's the picture!

Mr. Jones: You think you can do something for me, eh?

Mr. O'Donnell: I'll do my damnedest. I think I can.

Mr. Jones: You think you can to the point where you can solicit me to pay two thousand five hundred of my money in the hope that your thoughts are right?

Mr. O'Donnell: That's right.

I then told the gentleman that I would think over his proposal and made an appointment to see him again on the morrow. He stressed the desirability of keeping the matter confidential and handed me a receipt for $2,500.00 which actually had been prepared prior to his coming to my office, he apparently having felt secure in the confidence of his salesmanship ability with respect to the real thing the Democratic National Committee had to sell to one who, in his own words, had been put "in a spot!"

The Democratic National Committee, in a manner unknown to me, learned of the fact that I had made some kind of a record of O'Donnell's conversation with me. Newspapermen came to advise me that Mr. Forbes Morgan, Treasurer, stated that he held an affidavit from O'Donnell and the press carried that official's quotation that the affidavit was one "repudiating that alleged dictaphone record."

A denial of such sort struck me as really very

amusing. The characterization did not, of itself, deny the fact that a conversation had been held, neither did it deny the truth of what the record stated had been said. The very strange part of the quickly prepared denial, however, was that it actually had been issued prior to the time I had made the record public and before anyone possibly could have known what my record was to disclose!

Thinking that perhaps the affidavit "repudiating" the "record" had been made under the man's oath before the fact concerning the kind of record I actually had made was known, and to save anyone from committing the egregious error of denying the truth told by a simple phonographic needle as it took its story from a mechanical disc record, I eliminated further squirmings and wabblings of human tongues by summoning representatives of the press to my own office where, to clear all doubt as to the "alleged" record, I reproduced, on the loud speaker, the voices of O'Donnell and myself in the conversation. Press comment on the matter was widespread throughout the country.

I filed transcript of the recorded conversation with the United States Senate Committee on Campaign Expenditures, as well as with the United States District Attorney in New York City.

The Chairman of the Republican National Committee called upon the Senate Committee for action against those responsible for improper solicitations for campaign funds, but that Committee subsequently held, however, that no law had been violated in the premises.

The United States Attorney issued subpoena for two of my technicians who made the recordings, summoning these gentlemen as witnesses before a Federal Grand Jury, in a specified room of the Federal Building in New York. On appearing at the room at the time designated, the witnesses found no Grand Jury present. They then presented themselves to the United States Attorney who, through an assistant, instructed them to return on the following day, but to telephone before coming down to his office. On telephoning, according to instructions, the witnesses, on that second day scheduled for their appearance, were told to come to the United States Attorney's office on the following day, but, again, they were advised to telephone before making the trip.

In the afternoon, of the second day, the United States Attorney advised the press that the Grand Jury had found, on investigating the evidence presented, that no law had been violated.

When the witnesses telephoned on the third day, they were informed that they would not be needed.

I personally was never even invited to appear before any authority in connection with any phase of the investigation—if such, indeed ever took place.

The minority leader of the House of Representatives at Washington, the Honorable Bertrand H. Snell, requested a transcript of the recorded conversation with O'Donnell, and, on its receipt from me, filed it and other information with the Attorney General of the United States, asking whether the Department of Justice had instituted an investigation to determine whether Section 313 of the Federal Corrupt Practices Act had been violated by sales of books by the Democratic Committee. In Mr. Cummings' reply, finally made public under date of December 24th, 1937, Congressman Snell was advised that:

"A comprehensive study of the law and the facts has now been completed, and the conclusion has been reached that a criminal prosecution would not be warranted."

In about two weeks following the Democratic Committee's book-selling attempt, President Roosevelt, at the zenith of his popularity, was reelected and swept into office by a huge vote in that November Election of 1936.

CHAPTER XIX

Pax Vobiscum

My counsel and I had thought, during the fall of 1936, that possibly, for political reasons, the administration had been delaying deliberately my trial until after the November election. When, therefore, on the first of December, the trial again was postponed for another thirty days, my patience became thoroughly exhausted and I instructed counsel to oppose with his greatest vigor any further delay.

Accordingly, on the first of January, 1937, when the government once more asked further adjournment, my counsel demanded an immediate trial, pointing out to the judge the devastating effect upon me of the policy of delay which characterized the action of the United States Attorney. The trial, nevertheless, on the desire of the government, again was postponed for another thirty day period.

We concluded that surely we now would be given the privilege of a trial on the merits of the issue

that had been created by the charges in the indictment, which, strangely, had so quickly followed my
victory in the United States Supreme Court. We
therefore, at considerable cost, made full arrangements to proceed when the case next should be
called in the first week in February.

During all the intervening time, it should be
remembered that the "investigating" of my every
activity in the oil fields and elsewhere continued
without abatement. My clients were constantly in-
terviewed, my personal movements closely watched,
and the general "grind" of my business destruction
went forward with cruel effectiveness.

I was present and ready to proceed with my counsel in February when my case was again called.
To my amazement, anger and disgust, however, the
United States Attorney again requested adjournment for the traditional thirty days. Spirited clash-
ings between the attorneys of the respective sides
enlivened, for me, the short period of time it required for the judge, again, to allow another adjournment until the first week in March!

For one who never has been subjected to the
treatment suffered by me in my long struggle for
just an opportunity to prove my innocence of the
serious charges made against me by the government,
it must be difficult to realize the terrible effect of

such continuous delay. The worry incident to the unusual ordeal; the great expense of it all; the tantalizing effect of hope destroyed, courage shattered, confidence in all justice doubted—all combine to weaken even one's determination for strong defense against seemingly insuperable odds. "You can't lick the government" dins into the conscience of one so pressed, to write futility as answer to every question arising from one's own communion with one's own thoughts.

Additional burdens must be shouldered, however, and preparations anew went forward to what we, again, felt sure would be, as the columns call it, "My Day." When March rolled around, therefore, we were on hand in every expectation that my case, long under intensive preparation by several different agencies and departments of the government and whipped by the fury of several tempestuous squalls of publicity, would be called for trial.

When, again—and I thought to the very shame of the government—the United States Attorney, once more, with bland countenance, asked the Court to postpone my trial for still another thirty days, my counsel, Mr. Fischbach, goaded by his realization of the devastating effect upon me and my family of such seeming torture, eloquently demanded a surcease from the delaying tactics of the government. The judge once more, however, allowed the adjournment but, at this time, he notified the United States Attorney that if another request for delay beyond the April term of court were to be made, he would entertain a motion by my counsel to dismiss the indictment on the ground of "lack of prosecution."

The April term, therefore, saw my trial finally underway—one whole year following the decision of the Supreme Court in my favor, and the Grand Jury proceeding that produced the indictment which immediately thereafter was brought against me.

At the trial, my legal staff was headed by the Honorable Lloyd Paul Stryker, of New York, as Chief of Counsel—a gentleman characterized by a very high sense of honor; sincere and earnest in his endeavors; most capable in every detail of preparation and presentation; thoroughly genteel as an associate; tireless and fearless as well, in his work. He had as associates Mr. Fischbach and an Oklahoma oil lawyer.

If a perfect description of my trial were possible to flow from my humble pen, no outstanding or sensational occurrence would be related to quicken the pulse of the reader. It had been rumored that J. Edward Jones was to be convicted by "atmos-

phere"—and, as the history of the trial was recorded, "atmosphere" was about all that was offered in
the way of incriminating evidence.

Government witness after government witness
came forward—a crippled man exhibiting hideous
physical deformities, a deaf witness, an elderly, poor
lady nearing the century mark, a blind gentleman
—a parade to excite the sympathy of a jury of
twelve men!

But cross-examination of the government witnesses by Mr. Stryker, brought out the fact, time
and again, that such witnesses had no quarrel with
me—always had been dragged into the case by the
government itself and forced to appear against me!

The trial went on, day after day, and week after
week, until the United States Attorney had consumed three weeks of time in his efforts to convince
twelve men that I was a criminal and that the
world would be the better were I to make my
home in a penitentiary. "Atmosphere," however,
instead of thickening into something concrete, di-
luted itself perceptibly into nothing more substantial than very thin air. Indeed, my counsel advised
me at about three days before the government
finally rested, that if nothing were to be forthcoming of a nature more damaging than that which
already had been presented, they would be prepared

to advise me that the government's case had collapsed!

When, therefore, the United States Attorney actually rested his case without having unearthed anything to cause concern, my counsel, one and all, took the view that, since two and one-half years had been spent in preparing the case against me and three weeks had been required to present it, and, in their opinion, the government had failed even to "make a case," we could, in confidence, leave the matter to the Jury without putting on even one character witness or one scrap of paper in my defense.

I, at first, opposed the strategy recommended by my counsel as I was absorbed with the desire to relate to the jury a long list of items I had prepared for my defense. On listening to the analysis of the government's presentation which my counsel outlined to me, however, I came to the realization of the wisdom of the conclusion of my lawyers. My counsel, thereupon, surprised the courtroom audience, by permitting my case to be decided by the Jury from the one-sided presentation that three weeks of effort had produced for it.

With the record the government had made, therefore, punctuated only by cross-examination of the government's own witnesses, the Jury, after closing arguments, went out to decide my fate. They retired at exactly twenty minutes to twelve o'clock on the morning of April 30th, took plenty of time out for lunch and returned to their box precisely at twenty minutes past three that afternoon. In a few seconds thereafter, the foreman speaking to end a year old suspense, gladdened my heart and those of my counsel and many friends there present by uttering the words, "Not guilty!"

A full sense of all my responsibilities toward those in this life who look to me for happiness and support came upon me as I listened to the words that meant so much. My thoughts and feelings at that moment, however, are not for record.

Counting the decision in my case made by the Supreme Court of the United States as my first, the conclusion of my trial represented the second great victory in my long and costly struggle for individual rights and for my personal liberties. After April 30, 1937, only one major legal action with the Government remained for disposal—the old original injunction suit brought against me by the Securities and Exchange Commission in February, 1935. This suit resulted from the extraordinary exploits of John L. Flynn, together, of course, with his comrade, Rabell, whose good name had been protected when Flynn of the Securities and Exchange Commission took the stand as the sole witness for the defense at Rabell's trial. Be it remembered that Rabell it was who had sworn to the affidavit supporting the complaint the Commission had made against me. But Flynn, of the "Truth in Securities" Commission, under oath solemnly administered, swore before fellowman and Maker, that the honorable Commission did not intend to us the "affiant" as a government witness, thereby paving the way for the saving of his brother in crime-hunting, whose indictment thereupon was quickly dismissed by the honorable Judge.

As preparations now were begun by me for a trial on the merits of the old complaint the Commission had brought against me, the contacts naturally had between my counsel and those of the Commission brought about discussions that led to proffers of settlement of that case. Without needless discussion of a rather insipid and protracted series of negotiations, suffice to say that this legal action from which had come both the Supreme Court and my indictment cases, died a somewhat ignominious death. This occurred when the Securities and Exchange Commission signed, with me, a stipulation which, on whereasing the fact that certain allegations had been made by the Commission and also

the fact that such allegations had been denied by
me, carried an agreement that, because of such
profundities, the legal action instituted by the Commission was to be discontinued! This was done with
the agreement on my part also, that I would not
do in the future, that which I denied ever having
done in the past and which I never had professed a
desire to do at any time or at any place.

The stipulation was filed at New York on January 3rd, 1938, thereby ending without trial a
costly litigation and dissolving the temporary injunction to which I had voluntarily consented and
for the glory of which Mr. Flynn had celebrated
in such hilarious manner in my Biltmore quarters
on that famous night described in a previous chapter.

The "most effective weapon" was resorted to in
the following words announcing the event and issued as a publicity release in Washington by the
Securities and Exchange Commission.

"The Securities and Exchange Commission announced yesterday that a stipulation had been filed
in the United States District Court for the Southern District of New York in which J. Edward Jones
and four of his business associates agreed not to en-
gage in acts and practices alleged in an injunction
suit brought against them by the commission in

February, 1935, which allegations were denied by Mr. Jones and his associates.

Upon the filing of the stipulation the Securities and Exchange Commission discontinued the proceedings."

Thus ended three years of hard struggle in a battle of individualism against the arbitrary powers of a despotic tyranny in America. In a land governed by principles dedicated to freedom and liberty, petty vindictiveness ran riot to violate the cardinal precepts of such treasures. In a nation whose very foundations were built around the pillars of justice, political extortion and graft played hide-and-seek in the shadows of the White House. In a government that governed through agencies touted in "holier-than-thou" fashion as "truth" agencies, crookedness and "framings" were the weapons to besmear reputations honestly earned through years of effort. In a régime of men who usurped authority to write their own rules and regulations and who arbitrarily enforced such as though they were the legitimate laws of the land, "government by men" became the new Americana.

In circumstances such as these, it fell to my lot to fight the battle. It might well have been the reader of these lines who thus was honored. Indeed, he may, even yet, face, unexpectedly, that which came to me. But I sincerely hope that no power ever shall long exist in America, to smother opposition to evil forces that would destroy her heritage.

As I now weigh the results of my three victories, won with such great cost, never, I feel sure, to be fully measured—I regard the value of the principles written in the decision of the Supreme Court in protecting the rights of individuals in this country and, as well, the protection of individual liberty epitomized in the two words spoken by the foreman of my own Jury, as worth the sacrifices which I have made. The Latin inscription on the Great Seal of my home state of Kansas best represents this feeling—"*Ad Astra per Aspera.*"